John Haywood

THE PENGUIN
HISTORICAL ATLAS
OF THE VIKINGS

PENGUIN BOOKS

Published by the Penguin Group
Penguin Books Ltd, 27 Wrights Lane, London W8 5TZ, England
Penguin Putnam Inc., 375 Hudson Street, New York, New York 10014, USA
Penguin Books Australia Ltd, Ringwood, Victoria, Australia
Penguin Books Canada Ltd, 10 Alcorn Avenue, Toronto, Ontario, Canada M4V 3B2
Penguin Books (NZ) Ltd, 182–190 Wairau Road, Auckland 10, New Zealand

Penguin Books Ltd, Registered Offices: Harmondsworth, Middlesex, England

First published 1995
Published simultaneously by Viking
5 7 9 10 8 6 4

ISBN 0–14–0–51328–0

Foreword

Recent years have seen great changes in our historical understanding of the Vikings. The traditional image of the Vikings as nothing more than axe-yielding pirates bent on rape and pillage or conquest has been balanced by a new appreciation of peaceful Viking enterprise in the fields of trade, crafts, exploration and settlement. The wide-ranging activities of the Vikings—which extended from the Caspian Sea to North America—are suited to presentation in map form. It is the intention of this atlas to provide, as nearly as possible, a continuous series of maps covering the history of the Viking age from its pre-historic origins through to its end in the 12th century. The accompanying text is intended to highlight some of the major controversies and issues in the history of the Viking age rather than provide a comprehensive introduction to the subject. Some may feel that my approach has over-emphasized the Vikings' warlike activities at the expense of their more constructive enterprises. This is partly a consequence of practical considerations— war makes for more exciting history than peace and this is especially true where histori-cal maps are concerned—but it also reflects my own unease at the extent to which the importance of violence in the Viking age has been played down in many recent studies of the period. The Vikings could be a pretty rough crew when it suited them, and it suit-ed many of them very often in the period *c.* 800–1100, as the maps in this atlas make abundantly clear.

Although it is the author who tends to get most of the credit, any highly-illustrated book such as this is in reality a team effort and I would like to thank all the Swanston produc-tion team who have worked so hard to make it a success, especially Chris Schüler, the editor and Ralph Orme, the designer and illustrator. Any errors are solely the responsi-bility of the author. I would also like to thank Birgitte Lomborg in Copenhagen for help-ing with the picture research and Brian Dearden for allowing me to use unpublished material from his excavations at Pont de l'Arche. Finally, I would also like to acknowl-edge generally my enormous debt to the very many historians and archaeologists on whose original research I have depended so heavily in writing and researching this book.

John Haywood
Lancaster, 1995

for Charlotte

Contents

The Causes of the Viking Age

The Vikings burst quite suddenly into European history in the last decade of the 8th century with a series of terrifying attacks on the coasts of Britain, Ireland and Francia. For centuries, their Scandinavian homeland had been a remote region about which other Europeans knew little and cared less. Why then, after centuries of obscurity, did the Scandinavians take to the seas to make such a dramatic impact on the world?

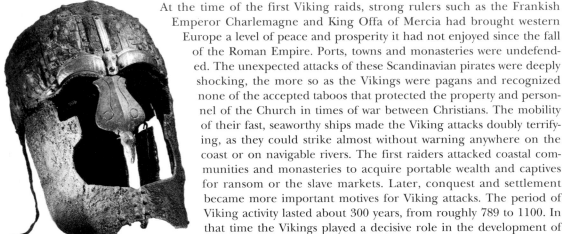

Above: *in the centuries leading up to the Viking Age, Scandinavia was ruled by warrior aristocrats whose power and status depended on war and plunder. Their prestige was enhanced by showy weapons and armour like this bronze-decorated iron helmet from a 7th-century ship burial at Vendel, Sweden.*

At the time of the first Viking raids, strong rulers such as the Frankish Emperor Charlemagne and King Offa of Mercia had brought western Europe a level of peace and prosperity it had not enjoyed since the fall of the Roman Empire. Ports, towns and monasteries were undefended. The unexpected attacks of these Scandinavian pirates were deeply shocking, the more so as the Vikings were pagans and recognized none of the accepted taboos that protected the property and personnel of the Church in times of war between Christians. The mobility of their fast, seaworthy ships made the Viking attacks doubly terrifying, as they could strike almost without warning anywhere on the coast or on navigable rivers. The first raiders attacked coastal communities and monasteries to acquire portable wealth and captives for ransom or the slave markets. Later, conquest and settlement became more important motives for Viking attacks. The period of Viking activity lasted about 300 years, from roughly 789 to 1100. In that time the Vikings played a decisive role in the development of much of western and eastern Europe, and were themselves transformed from pagan barbarians to Christian Europeans.

The geographical range of Viking activity was enormous, spanning most of the known world and going some way beyond it. Viking raids affected the whole coastline of western Europe, and even North Africa and the Mediterranean were not secure from attack. In the east the Vikings sailed down the great rivers of Russia to cross the Black Sea and the Caspian Sea to attack Constantinople and the Abbasid Caliphate. Vikings settled extensively in the British Isles, Normandy and, to a lesser extent, in Russia but they also pushed at the limits of the known world, crossing the North Atlantic to settle in the uninhabited Faeroe Islands, Iceland and Greenland and to discover, but fail to settle, North America. Viking traders and hunters extended the limits of the known world even further, sailing far into the Arctic waters of the White Sea and exploring the west coast of Greenland as far north as Melville Bay in search of walrus ivory and hides. Faced with this far-flung activity it is all too easy to forget that Scandinavia itself was also the scene of a great deal of Viking raiding and piracy. The Viking expansion was in no way a Scandinavian campaign against the rest of the world: Vikings were quite happy to plunder their own kind if the opportunity arose.

The term "Viking" has come to be applied to all Scandinavians of the period, but in the Viking age itself the term *víkingr* applied only to someone who went *í víking*, that is plundering. In this sense, most Viking-age Scandinavians were not Vikings at all, but peaceful farmers and craftsmen who stayed quietly at home all their lives. For many others, being a Viking was just an occupation they resorted to for long enough to raise the money to buy, or otherwise acquire, a farm and settle down. Nor were those who went viking necessarily exclusively Scandinavian: Irishmen, Anglo-Saxons, Franks, Bretons and Slavs all joined in Viking raids at times. Though it has led to unneccessary controversy on some important aspects of the history of the Viking age (the question of Viking violence, for example), the wider use of "Viking" is too well established to insist on using the word only in the narrow meaning of "pirate".

The Wrath of God

The Vikings' victims had little difficulty explaining the raids: they were God's punishment on a sinful people. Archbishop Wulfstan of York expressed this view eloquently in his *Sermon of the Wolf to the English*, written after Svein Forkbeard's victory over the English in 1014: "Things have not gone well now for a long time at home or abroad, but there has been devastation and persecution in every district again and again, and the English have been for a long time now completely defeated and too greatly disheartened through God's anger; and the pirates so strong with God's consent that often in battle one puts to flight ten, and sometimes less, sometimes more, all because of our sins ... what else is there in all these events except God's anger clear and visible over his people?" (tr. D. Whitelock, *English Historical Documents I*, Oxford 1979).

Modern historians have found the Viking age harder to explain. Land-hunger caused by a growing population has often been proposed as a cause of the Viking expansion. The population of Scandinavia certainly was rising in the centuries before the first raids, and it continued to do so during and after the Viking age. The area under cultivation was expanding, new settlements were created and iron production increased to meet the demand for tools. Scandinavia has relatively little good arable land and it might be expected that the pressure of a rising population would soon be felt. Norway has not been self-sufficient in food since the Middle Ages, and both Norway and Sweden have seen considerable emigration in periods of population growth in recent historical times. There is evidence of migrations out of Scandinavia before the Viking age. The Cimbri and Teutones who invaded the Roman Empire in 113 BC probably originated in Jutland, while many of the Germanic peoples—including the Goths, Burgundians and Vandals—who invaded the Roman Empire in the 5th century AD had traditions that they had originally lived in Scandinavia. To the 6th-century Gothic historian Jordanes, Scandinavia was the "womb of peoples". There was also considerable emigration out of Scandinavia during the Viking age, and it may be significant that the earliest Scandinavian settlements, dating from the early to mid-9th century, were made by Norwegians in the northern and western isles of Scotland and the Faeroe islands.

But the first wave of Vikings was dominated by raiders, not settlers—more than 80 years passed before any major settlements were made. Iceland was only settled in 870s, and the Danish settlement of eastern England began around the same time. Norwegians did not begin to settle in northwest England until around 900, and the Danish settlement of Normandy dates from 911. Despite the intensity of Viking raiding in Ireland, there were never any extensive Scandinavian settlements there, while the Rus (Swedes) who ruled in eastern Europe were a small warrior-elite; their subjects remained overwhelmingly Slav. Land-hunger, then, can hardly have been the main cause of the Viking expansion—it is more likely that it was the success of the

Above: **This bronze statuette of the Buddha somehow found its way from northern India to Helgö in Sweden in the 6th or 7th century AD. Finds like this are evidence that the Scandinavians already had wide-ranging trade contacts before the Viking age.**

Viking attacks that opened the way for Scandinavian settlement.

Another reason put forward for the Viking explosion is Scandinavian ship-building. The 8th century, it has been argued, saw the Scandinavians perfect the technology of the seagoing sailing ship: before this time they had relied on large rowing boats which, while suitable for piracy in sheltered coastal waters, were inadequate for long-distance raiding. The adoption of the sail, therefore, opened up enormous new opportunities for piracy which the Scandinavians were quick to exploit. It is true that without seaworthy ships the Viking expansion could not have happened, but this is not the same thing as demonstrating that they were a cause of it. Though no pre-Viking ship yet discovered in Scandinavia has provided any evidence of the use of the sail, late 7th-century stone carvings from the Baltic island of Gotland do show sailing ships, as does a recently discovered 7th-century stone carving from Jutland. It is therefore possible that the Scandinavians had suitable ships for some time before the start of Viking raiding. Moreover, sea-raids out of Scandinavia were not completely unknown before the Viking age, the earliest recorded one being a raid of the Heruls (from Jutland) on the lower Rhine in AD 287.

Traders and Raiders

A more important factor in the Viking expansion was probably trade: it is certainly the most convincing explanation of the origins of the Swedish expansion to the east. The 8th century was a time of political stability in western Europe. The resulting economic recovery led to an increase in trade with Scandinavia, which was an important source of luxury goods such as furs, amber and walrus ivory, and probably of more mundane products such as hides. By the mid 8th century the Swedes had already begun to establish themselves in settlements such as Staraja Ladoga, east of the Baltic. These are best explained as bases for the collection of tribute in furs, which the Swedes could then use to supply the western European market. At about the same time, Arab merchants were penetrating eastern Europe from the south along the Volga and the Don. As a result, high quality Arabic silver coins known as *dirhems* began to circulate in eastern Europe, giving the Swedes an incentive to push further east to tap directly into a new and lucrative market.

The existence of piracy implies the presence of something worth plundering, so the increase in trade with western Europe may also have encouraged Viking raiding. Viking piracy, preying on merchant ships, may have been endemic in the Baltic long before it spilled over into the North Sea. Even the earliest Viking raiders in the west seem to have known which places to attack, and it was probably on peaceful merchant voyages that the Scandinavians first learned about western Europe's rich and unguarded ports and coastal monasteries. The Scandinavians were certainly known to the Anglo-Saxons and Franks before they began raiding; according to the Northumbrian scholar Alcuin, writing after the sack of Lindisfarne in 793, his countrymen were so familiar with them that they had even adopted their hairstyles. The circumstances of another early Viking raid, on Portland *c.*789, also suggests that the Anglo-Saxons were already familiar with Scandinavian merchants. Three ships from Hörthaland (in Norway) arrived at the port. The king's reeve Beaduheard, believing them to be merchants, ordered the crews to go to the royal residence at Dorchester: Beaduheard was killed for his trouble. Small-scale pirate raids like this continued to prey on coastal settlements and merchant shipping until the 12th century.

Rivals and Exiles

Many Viking leaders were royal exiles, and this points to another reason for the Viking expansion. Immediately before and during the Viking age, Scandinavian society was going through major changes which saw the progressive centralization of power in fewer and fewer hands. However, Scandinavian society had a relatively numerous class of men who, through the possession of royal blood, could aspire to kingship. Competition for power was intense, and succession disputes were frequent and bloody. For the losers in these struggles, there was little choice but to go into exile. Some of these exiles, like Olaf Tryggvason in the 10th century, went raiding to build up their wealth and reputation. This would gain them a following of warriors, who would support a bid for power at home. Even the great Cnut was successful abroad before he won power in Denmark.

Others, like Erik Bloodaxe, may have decided that if they could not rule at home, they would rule abroad. Erik, driven off the Norwegian throne by his brother, sought a kingdom overseas in compensation, establishing himself as the King of York in 948. Ivar, Halfdan and the other leaders of the Great Army that invaded England in 865 seem to have been intent on establishing overseas kingdoms from the start of their careers. The Danish King Svein Forkbeard was an example of another kind of leader. Recognizing the threat successful Vikings could pose to his own position, he led his own plundering raids to overawe potential rivals with his wealth and military prowess. As royal power became more entrenched in the 11th century, the Scandinavian nations evolved into medieval European kingdoms. Their rulers could depend on reliable institutionalized sources of wealth-gathering, such as taxes and tolls, and the importance of plunder as a means of buying support declined. There was no longer such a strong incentive to go raiding, and the Viking age faded away.

Right: *This silver coin was struck at the Channel port of Quentovic during the reign of the Frankish Emperor Charlemagne (769–814). The trading ship in the design reflects the growing commercial prosperity of western Europe at the time. By the end of the 8th century the rich pickings were encouraging the Scandinavians to turn to piracy.*

Timeline: AD 1–824

SCANDINAVIA	BRITAIN AND IRELAND	WESTERN EUROPE	THE EAST	WORLD EVENTS
c. AD 1–400 warrior aristocracy emerges in southern Scandinavia *c.* 400–600 forts built at Eketorp and Ismantorp on Öland. Angles and Jutes migrate to Britain				
				410 Visigoths sack Rome. Emperor Honorius tells Britons to fend for themselves
	c. 425–500 Saxons migrate to Britain			
		c. 455 & 460 Heruls raid Spain		
				476 fall of Roman Empire in west 482 Clovis king of Franks
c. 550 Gothic writer Jordanes records locations of Scandinavian peoples				
				511 Clovis dies; Frankish kingdom divided
		c. 528 Hygelac king of the Geats raids Frisia and the Rhine		
				535 Byzantine reconquest of Italy begins
		c. 570 Danes raid Frisia		
c. 600–800 kingdoms develop in Denmark, Norway and Sweden	597 St Augustine begins conversion of Anglo-Saxons			
				622 Mohammed's flight *(hijra)* from Mecca begins Muslim era
	635 St Aidan founds monastery on Lindisfarne			642 Muslims conquer Egypt
	664 Synod of Whitby ensures dominance of Roman church in England			
c. 700 ship burial at Vendel				711 Muslims begin conquest of Spain
c. 720 Angantyr king of Denmark *c.* 725 Willibrord leads the first Christian mission to Scandinavia 726 military canal built at Kanhave, Denmark				
737 First phase of Danevirke rampart completed				732 Frankish King Charles Martel halts Muslim advance near Poitiers
			c. 750 Swedes established at Staraja Ladoga	750 Umayyad Caliphate overthrown by Abassid dynasty; Umayyad exiles take over Spain
	c. 789 Norwegian Vikings attack Portland 793 Vikings plunder monastery of Lindisfarne 795 First recorded Viking raids on Scotland and Ireland			
		799 Vikings raid Aquitaine 800 Charlemagne organizes defences against Vikings		800 Charlemagne crowned emperor in Rome
808 Godfred king of the Danes destroys Slav town of Reric and transfers merchants to Hedeby. Danevirke extended 810 Godfred murdered		810 King Godfred raids Frisia		
813 Danish kings campaign to re-establish their authority in Vestfold, Norway				814 death of Charlemagne; succeeded by Louis the Pious
823-4 Ebo, archbishop of Reims, makes mission to Denmark				

AD 825–906

SCANDINAVIA	BRITAIN AND IRELAND	WESTERN EUROPE	THE EAST	WORLD EVENTS
c. 825 Danish coinage in Hedeby begins 826 Danish King Harald Klak baptized at Mainz. Ansgar's first mission to Denmark 829-30 Ansgar's first mission to the Svear at Birka	*c.* 825 Irish monks driven out of Faeroes by Vikings			827 Muslims invade Sicily 830-4 civil war in Carolingian empire
	832 Armagh raided three times in one month 839-40 Vikings winter in Ireland for the first time 841 Viking base established at Dublin	834-7 Dorestad raided annually 842 Vikings winter in Francia for the first time 843-85 Frisia under intermittent Danish control 844 First Viking raid on Spain 845 Hamburg and Paris sacked. First Danegeld paid by Franks	839 Swedes reach Constantinople	843 Carolingian empire partitioned
850 Ansgar builds churches at Ribe and Hedeby 852-4 Ansgar's second mission to the Svear 854 Horik, king of Denmark, killed in civil war *c.* 860 Gardar the Swede explores coast of Iceland	850 Vikings winter for the first time in England	859-62 Bjorn Ironsides and Hastein raid in Mediterranean *c.* 862 Charles the Bald orders construction of fortified bridges against Vikings	860 Rus attack Constantinople for the first time *c.* 862 Rurik becomes ruler of Novgorod. Askold and Dir seize Kiev	846 Muslim pirates sack Vatican *c.* 850 Spanish Christians push Muslims back to R. Duero *c.* 863 Byzantine missionaries Cyril and Methodius sent to convert Slavs. Schism between Orthodox and western churches
c. 870-930 Vikings settle Iceland	865 Danish Great Army invades England 867 Danes capture York 870 Danes conquer East Anglia *c.* 870 Earldom of Orkney established 871–99 Alfred king of Wessex 874-914 "Forty Years Rest" in Ireland 876-9 initial Danish settlement in England 878 Alfred defeats Danes at Edington. Treaty of Wedmore establishes Danelaw			
c. 885-900 Harald Finehair wins the battle of Hafrsfjord uniting most of Norway under his rule	886 London recaptured from Danes	885-6 Vikings besiege Paris	*c.* 882 Oleg unites Novgorod and Kiev	888 Final breakup of the Carolingian empire. Odo king of West Franks, Arnulf king of East
c. 900 Norwegian settlement in northwest England 902 Vikings expelled from Dublin 902-54 West Saxon conquest of Danelaw		891 Vikings defeated by Arnulf at the Dyle		*c.* 900 revival of Byzantine power in Turkey and the Balkans

Timeline: AD 907–1024

SCANDINAVIA	BRITAIN AND IRELAND	WESTERN EUROPE	THE EAST	WORLD EVENTS
			907 Rus attack Constantinople 911 Rus make treaty with Byzantines 912-13 Viking raiders in Caspian Sea	
		911 Rollo founds Normandy		
		914-36 Vikings occupy Brittany		
	917 Vikings recapture Dublin			
930 Icelandic Althing founded 934 Danes defeated by Henry the Fowler, king of Germany				
				936–73 Otto the Great emperor of Germany
	937 English defeat Norse-Scottish alliance at battle of Brunanburh		941 Igor unsuccessfully beseiges Constantinople and makes treaty. Rus becoming assimilated into Slavic population	941 Hugh Capet king of France
948 bishops appointed to Ribe, Hedeby and Arhus	954 Erik Bloodaxe killed at Stainmore: end of Viking kingdom of York			
958 death of Gorm the Old 960 Harald Bluetooth restores Danish dominance in Norway			964-71 Svyatoslav campaigns against Bulgars, Khazars and Byzantines	
c. 965 Harald converts Danes to Christianity 968 Danevirke refortified against German invasion c. 970 Sigtuna founded 974-81 Hedeby under German occupation				c. 965 Muslim silver mines exhausted
				978 war between East and West Franks. Æthelræd king of England (to 1016)
c. 980 round forts built in Denmark 986 Erik the Red begins settlement of Greenland	980 Viking raids on England recommence		c. 980 Varangian guard formed at Constantinople	
			988 Vladimir, prince of Kiev, converts to Orthodox Christianity	
	991 Olaf Tryggvason defeats English at Maldon			
995 Olaf Tryggvason unites Norway. Olof Skötkonung becomes first king of both Svear and Götar 1000 conversion of Iceland. Olaf Tryggvason killed at battle of Svöld c. 1000 voyages to Vinland				
		1002 Svein Forkbeard uses Normandy as base to attack England		1002 Muslim Caliphate of Cordoba collapses into petty states
	1014 Brian Boru defeats alliance of Leinster and Norse at Clontarf. Svein Forkbeard conquers England			
1015 Olaf Haraldsson conquers Norway	1016-35 Cnut king of England			
1027 first stone church in Denmark built at Roskilde			1019–54 zenith of Kievan power	
1030 Olaf Haraldsson killed at battle of Stiklestad. He is soon regarded as a saint	c. 1030-5 battle of Tarbet Ness: Earl Thorfinn of Orkney wins control over most of northern Scotland			
	1042 end of Danish rule in England		1041 Ingvar the Widefarer's expedition to the east	1042–66 Edward the Confessor king of England

AD 1043–1500

SCANDINAVIA	BRITAIN AND IRELAND	WESTERN EUROPE	THE EAST	WORLD EVENTS
1043 Magnus the Good defeats Wends at battle of Lyrskov Heath near Hedeby 1047-64 conflict between Harald Hardrada of Norway and Svein Estrithson of Denmark			1043 last Rus attack on Constantinople	
	c. 1050 bishopric founded in Orkney			1055 Seljuk Turks take Baghdad
	1066 Harald Hardrada killed at Stamford Bridge. Battle of Hastings 1069 Svein Estrithson invades England			
	1075 last Danish invasion of England 1079 battle of Skyhill, Isle of Man: Godred Crovan unites Man and Hebrides	1071 Normans expand into southern Italy		1071 Seljuks defeat Byzantines at Manzikert
1085 oldest known grant of land to the church in Scandinavia. Cnut IV abandons planned expedition to England				1085 King Alfonso I of Leon takes Toledo from Muslims
	1095 Malcolm Canmore, king of Scotland, recognizes Norwegian sovereignty over Hebrides 1103 Magnus Barelegs, king of Norway, killed raiding Ulster			1095-9 First Crusade
1107-11 Norwegian king Sigurd the Jerusalem-farer leads crusade to Holy Land 1122-33 Ari Thorgilsson writes Islendingabók (the Book of the Icelanders) 1147 Danes attack pagan Wends as part of Second Crusade				1147–8 Second Crusade
1155–70 civil wars in Scandinavia	1153 King Harald Eystein raids east coast of England from Norway			1155 Frederick Barbarossa crowned emperor
1163 first coronation in Scandinavia: Magnus Erlingsson crowned king of Norway 1169 Danes conquer Rügen Island and begin expansion into Baltic	1156 Somerled wins southern Hebrides from Godred II of Man			
	1170 Anglo-Normans conquer Dublin			1187 Saladin takes Jersualem 1204 Fourth Crusade takes Constantinople 1237–42 Mongols invade eastern Europe
1261 Greenland comes under direct rule from Norway 1263 Iceland comes under Norwegian rule	1263 Scots defeat Hakon IV at Largs 1266 Norway cedes Man and Hebrides to Scotland		1271 end of Rurik dynasty in Rus	
1341 Eskimos occupy Western Settlement, Greenland				1337 outbreak of Hundred Years War between England and France
1380 Eskimos occupy Middle Settlement, Greenland				1347 Black Death in Europe
late 15th century last Norse Greenland colony becomes extinct	1469 Denmark cedes Orkney and Shetland to Scotland			1453 Ottoman Turks take Constantinople. End of Hundred Years War

I: The Origins of the Vikings

The Vikings' way of life was shaped by their Scandinavian homeland. Its harsh environment, seafaring tradition and the power struggles between rival warlords led the Scandinavians to plunder their richer neighbours to the south.

The homeland of the Vikings was the three modern Scandinavian countries: Denmark, Norway and Sweden. Scandinavia is a vast region stretching some 1200 miles (2000km) from the neck of the Jutland peninsula in the south to North Cape well beyond the Arctic Circle. Only in the far north and south does Scandinavia lack clearly defined borders. In the north Scandinavia merges seamlessly into the tundras of north Russia. Scandinavia's short southern land frontier across the neck of the Jutland has always been hard to define, and its present position dates only from 1920. However, southern Jutland has extensive areas of infertile soils and until the advent of modern agricultural methods it was a sparsely populated area which acted as a natural buffer zone between the German peoples to the south and the Scandinavians to the north.

Below: The circular stone fort of Gråborg is the largest of many built on Öland during the Migration Period, a time of intense competition between rival chiefdoms. The fort was pressed into service again in the late Viking period as a refuge against Wendish pirates.

Southern Scandinavia—Jutland, the Danish islands and Sweden south of the Southern Uplands—is essentially a low-lying extension of the north European plain. Though there are large areas of infertile sands deposited by rivers of meltwater from ice sheets during the last Ice Age, this area has the best soils in Scandinavia. Though rarely rising above 1000 feet (300m), the Swedish Southern Uplands, an area of lakes, bogs and dense forest, were a significant obstacle to travel and formed a natural barrier between the Danes and the Swedes until the 17th century.

Norway, on the west of the Scandinavian peninsula, is completely dominated by a long range of ancient fold mountains known in Viking times as "The Keel". These rise steeply from the sea in the west and decline gradually in the southeast to the Gulf of Bothnia and the lowlands around Lake Vänern and Lake Mälaren in Sweden. The west coast is indented with deep fjords, some of which penetrate over a hundred miles inland. Off the coast are chains of islands and reefs, the Skerry Guard, which form a sheltered coastal passage for shipping. This sea route to the north, the "North Way", gave Norway its name. During the Ice Age the Scandinavian peninsula was very heavily glaciated, and the landscape of Norway and northern Sweden has been scoured by ice. Soils are generally thin, stoney, waterlogged and infertile: only in the Trondelag, around Oslo Fjord and the plains around Lake Vänern and Lake Mälaren are there extensive areas of fertile soils. During the Ice Age, the weight of the Scandinavian ice cap depressed the land surface. Since the ice cap melted at the end of the Ice Age, the land—relieved of the huge weight of ice—has been steadily rising. As a result, the coastline has receded since Viking times. This is most evident in central Sweden: in Viking times Lake Mälaren was an inlet of the sea offering easy access to the interior. The relative fall in sea level was a contributory factor in the decline of some Viking age ports and trade centres such as Birka on Lake Mälaren and Kaupang on Oslo Fjord, which gradually became more and more difficult to reach by ship.

Climate and Agriculture

The climate of Scandinavia is maritime in the west and continental in the east. Because of the moderating influence of the Gulf Stream the Norwegian coast has cool summers and, for its latitude, mild winters. It is a poor climate for growing grain, but agriculture based on pastoralism is possible even in the Lofoten Islands over 120 miles (192km) north of the Arctic Circle. Norwegian waters remain ice free throughout the year. Inland the climate deteriorates rapidly and winters in the mountains are severe, with heavy snowfalls. However, the mountains were an important source of summer grazing and of bog-iron ore. Most of Sweden lies in the rain shadow of the Norwegian mountains, and the climate is much drier. Summers are warm and sunny, but Sweden's remoteness from the warming influence of the Gulf Stream means that winters can be severe, and sea ice can close the Baltic to shipping for several weeks or even months each year. The climate of Denmark and southernmost Sweden shows both maritime and continental influences, with moderate rainfall, warm summers and cold but not severe winters. The climate is well suited to pastoral and arable farming which, combined with the best soils in Scandinavia, has always made Denmark and southern Sweden the richest farming region in Scandinavia.

The geography of Scandinavia has always exerted an influence on its historical development, most obviously in the field of communications. Mountains, forests and bogs have always made overland travel difficult in the Scandinavian peninsula: most long-distance overland travel took place in the winter when the ground was frozen hard. However, Scandinavia is well provided with sheltered coastal waters, fjords, lakes and navigable rivers; from the Stone Age, boats and ships became the most important means of transport, so the Vikings were heirs to a long tradition of seafaring and shipbuilding. The poverty of the soils in much of Scandinavia added another incentive for seafaring as fishing, seal and walrus hunting and trade all offered attractive alternatives, or at least supplements, to a hard living on

Above: The importance of ships and the sea is evident throughout Scandinavian prehistoric art, religion and burial customs. Chieftains were frequently buried in ships, or within an enclosure of stones arranged to form the outline of a ship, as in this Bronze Age burial in Gotland.

the land. The shortage of good soils may also have led to land hunger at times of population growth, and bred a willingness to emigrate.

The nature of the land also had a great effect on the political development of Scandinavia. Communication by both land and sea were easiest in Denmark and southern Sweden. This region had the best soils and climate, so it could support the densest population. As a result, it was the first area of Scandinavia to see the formation of a unified state; this explains why Denmark, in spite of its small size, remained the leading Scandinavian kingdom until the 17th century. Norway by contrast has a highly fragmented geography which naturally lends itself to the formation of strong local identities. The two largest areas of good farming land, and hence the wealthiest and most densely populated parts of Norway, were the Trondelag and the Oslo Fjord region. Since they are widely separated, they developed as rival power centres, delaying the unification of the country.

The Early Scandinavians

The first human inhabitants of Scandinavia were nomadic hunters who followed the seasonal migrations of reindeer herds across what was then the north German tundra into southern Scandinavia at the height of the last glaciation around 11,000 BC. Permanent human settlement in Scandinavia began around 8000 years ago as bands of hunter-gatherers moved north in the wake of the retreating ice sheets. These bands moved between semi-permanent camps every few months to exploit a wide range of seasonal animal and plant foods. There is no convincing evidence of any later migrations into Scandinavia, so it seems likely that the Vikings were the direct descendants of these hunter-gatherers. Around 4000 BC the early Scandinavians adopted agriculture, probably as a result of contacts with farming peoples to the south. Around 2000 BC flint tools began to be replaced by bronze, and iron tools began to appear c. 500 BC. The Stone Age (Neolithic) farmers lived in isolated family farms, but impressive megalithic communal tombs stand as monuments to some sort of common identity. By the Bronze Age, in the more fertile areas at least, farms were beginning to cluster together in villages. The presence of a single large dwelling among otherwise smaller dwellings suggests that villages were dominated by a headman or chief. Small numbers of richly furnished graves also point to the emergence of a ruling class in Bronze-Age Scandinavia. This process of increasing social stratification continued throughout the Scandinavian Iron Age (c. 500 BC –AD 1000).

The beginning of the Early Iron Age (500 BC–AD 1) appears to have been marked by a decline in population, perhaps caused by climatic deterioration, but the population was growing again by the end of the period and would continue to do so throughout the remainder of the Iron Age. Some of the most important finds of this period are votive offerings of weapons, cauldrons, pottery and food, as well as several human sacrificial victims, deposited in bogs and superbly preserved by the acid conditions.

It was in the Roman Iron Age (AD 1–400) and the succeeding Germanic Iron Age (400–800) that Scandinavian society developed its familiar Viking characteristics. Because of the virtual absence of literary sources, it is impossible to reconstruct the political and social changes of the period in any detail, but they can be drawn in outline on the basis of archaeological evidence and by comparison with the better-documented German peoples to the south.

In the Roman Iron Age the objects found in votive deposits are almost exclusively weapons, presumably thank offerings for victory in battle. The presence, especially in Denmark, of many Roman weapons in these offerings suggests that the Scandinavians were often engaged in battle with the German tribes to the south, who were in direct contact with the Roman Empire. The increasing importance of war in society is also indicated by the appearance of warrior graves furnished with weapons, suggesting that Scandinavian society was now dominated by a warrior elite. A smaller number of graves containing weapons and prestige luxury goods suggests that this warrior elite included a class of chieftains or, perhaps, petty kings. Finds of everyday Roman objects like pottery and coins alongside luxury goods like glass, silverware and jewellery show that there were direct or indirect trade links between Scandinavia and the Roman world. Seasonal trading centres, often associated with cult centres, such as Lundeborg in Denmark, sprang up. Finds of Roman goods are, not surprisingly, most common in southern Scandinavia but they are not evenly distributed: a notable concen-

Below: Human sacrifice was common in Iron Age Scandinavia. The victims' bodies were placed with other offerings to the gods in peat bogs, where the chemicals in the ground have preserved them in remarkable condition. Tollund man was found in Jutland, with the hide rope used to hang him still in place around his neck.

Above: *The centuries immediately preceding the outbreak of Viking raiding saw great development in Scandinavian shipbuilding techniques. This 8th century carved picture stone from Gotland shows an early sailing ship alongside mythological scenes.*

tration in Sjælland suggests that in the late Roman Iron Age a centralized authority, probably a kingdom, had developed here with enough power to control trade over a wide area.

The indirect cause of these social changes was probably the Roman influence on the German tribes to the south. Through a combination of trade, subsidy, plunder and payment for mercenary services, the German tribes in direct contact with the Romans were greatly enriched, and this must have made them an attractive target for raiding by their poorer neighbours to the north. Those who were most successful in these raids would soon be set apart from the rest of society by their greater wealth and status. It is likely that the Roman Iron Age saw the development of the *comitatus* or war band, an institution which is well attested among the German tribes in this period. The *comitatus* was made up of young warriors who became the followers of a successful chieftain or king. In return for their loyalty the warriors expected to be rewarded, and the war band would only stay together as long as the leader had the wealth to reward them. Though a leader could gather wealth through peaceful means such as landownership or by controlling trade, military expeditions to win plunder and tribute were usually more effective. This created a very competitive, predatory society, where success in war was the key to power and status. It also led to the concentration of power in fewer and fewer hands and to the merging of tribes, either voluntarily to wage war or resist aggression more effectively, or because a weaker tribe had been conquered by a stronger. It was probably in this way, for example, that the Danes emerged as the dominant people of southern Scandinavia by the 6th century.

The Early Germanic Iron Age or Migration Period (400–600) saw the proliferation of fortifications across Scandinavia; over 1500 are known. As Scandinavia suffered no invasions from outside in this period these fortifications should be seen as evidence of internal insecurity born of these intense power struggles. Many of these fortifications were probably the centres of chieftaincies and local kingdoms. There is also evidence of a tendency for settlement to move away from the coasts, a sign that piracy was rife. Though, no doubt, unreliable in detail, the early historical traditions of the Scandinavians hold that this was indeed a period of constant conflict between competing tribes. Though Scandinavia escaped invasion during the Migration Period, the Jutland tribes of the Angles and Jutes joined the Saxons in migrating to Britain in the 5th century. What prompted this migration is not known, but it is possible that they were under pressure from neighbouring peoples.

The Rise of Kingdoms

The archaeological evidence points to the development of powerful regional kingdoms in the Late Germanic Iron Age (600–800), the last period of the Scandinavian Iron Age before the Viking age. One such kingdom was centred in Uppland in Sweden, north of Lake Mälaren, around the pagan cult centre of Gamla Uppsala. Nearby are cemeteries at Vendel and Valsgärde containing burials with exceptionally rich furnishings, including ships and fine armour. These were probably cemeteries of the royal dynasty of the Svear people from whom Sweden would take its name. Jutland was the centre of another early kingdom, though the evidence here comes from large scale defence works rather than burials.

In 726, a canal was built through an isthmus on the island of Samsø, probably to regulate shipping and in 737 an earthwork barrier —the Danevirke— was built across the neck of the Jutland peninsula. (The reason we have such precise dates is because timbers can be dated by dendrochronology, the study of their ring patterns). Both were major projects, and whoever built them must have been able to command labour and resources over a wide area. At around the same time a trading place at Ribe was founded. All of these projects were perhaps the responsibility of King Angantyr, who St Willibrord met on a mission to Jutland in the early 8th century. Angantyr is described as king of the Danes, but whether this means all of them or just the Danes in Jutland is uncertain: the latter seems more likely. The rich burial mounds at Borre and Oseberg in Vestfold suggest the development of an emergent kingdom in this part of Norway immediately before the Viking Age. In the course of the Viking age these primitive and precarious states would be forged into the medieval kingdoms of Denmark, Sweden and Norway.

Right: *The wealth and splendour of the late Iron Age Scandinavian aristocracy is evident from this jewelled Vendel-style brooch from Aker, Norway.*

The Scandinavian Environment

Scandinavia's history has always been shaped by its landscape, especially its relationship with the sea.

"The interior is washed and encompassed by the Ocean… Denmark is cut in pieces by the intervening waves… and has but few portions of firm and continuous territory… Of all these Jutland, being the largest and first settled, holds the chief place in the Danish kingdom."

Saxo Grammaticus, *History of the Danes, c. 1200*

Two contrasting Scandinavian landscapes; the steep, rocky chasm of Norway's Geiranger Fjord (right), *and the pastoral landscape of Brendeshøj in Denmark, with a view across the Sejero Bvgt to Sjaellands Odde* (below).

Despite its northerly latitude, Scandinavia has a surprisingly mild climate thanks to the warming Gulf Stream. The coastal areas of Norway, though wet, are mild. Sweden has severe winters, but warm, dry summers compensate. Agriculture is restricted by the scarcity of suitable soils. Denmark, the smallest country, has the highest proportion of arable land, making the Danes the wealthiest, most numerous and most politically advanced of the Scandinavians in the Viking age. Norway has only two extensive areas of farmland: around Trondheim in the north and Oslo Fjord in the south. Because of the great distance and poor communications between them, they became rival power centres, delaying the creation of a unified Norwegian kingdom until the 12th century. In times of rapid population growth, shortage of arable land became serious; the Viking age was just one of many periods in which Scandinavians migrated in search of land to farm.

The sea was an important fact of life. The poverty of the land made fishing an essential source of food, and the geography of the region meant that it was often easier to travel by water than by land. Boat-building and seamanship were essential skills, most obviously for the island-dwelling Danes. In Norway the mountainous terrain and deeply indented coastline made inland travel arduous; sailing along the sheltered fjords was far quicker and safer. In Sweden, rivers and lakes offered the best routes into the densely forested country; long-distance travel overland mainly took place in winter, when the bogs and rivers were frozen.

The pattern of Viking activity is closely related to the locations of the Scandinavian peoples. Norwegian expansion was mostly to the west: to Scotland, Ireland, the Faeroe Islands, Iceland and ultimately to Greenland and North America. The Danes' territory straddled the main sea route from the Baltic to the Rhine, so it is not surprising they first concentrated on Frisia and then spread to England and Francia. Swedes, cut off from the western seas by the Danes and Norwegians, had only one outlet: east, along the great rivers that led into the heartlands of Russia.

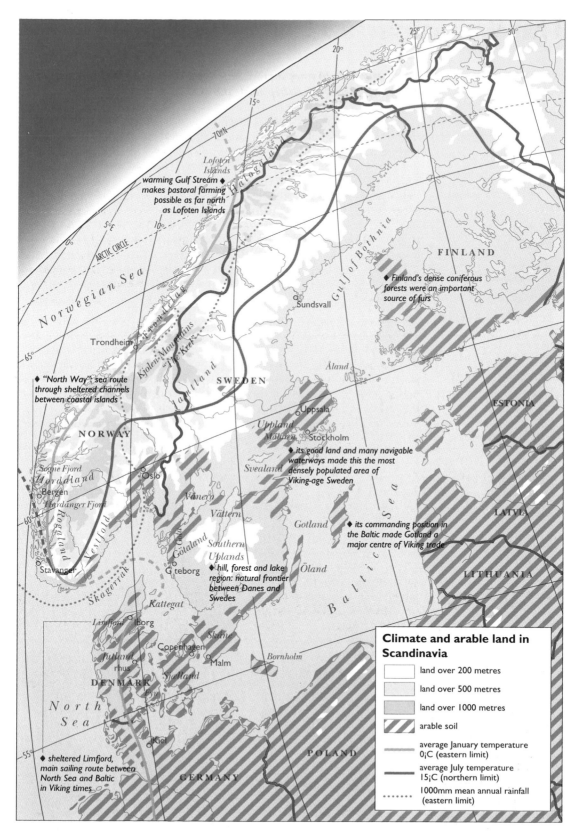

warming Gulf Stream ♦
makes pastoral farming
possible as far north
as Lofoten Islands

Lofoten
Islands

♦ Finland's dense coniferous
forests were an important
source of furs

FINLAND

Norwegian Sea

Sundsvall

Gulf of Bothnia

ARCTIC CIRCLE

Trondheim

Jämtland

♦ "North Way": sea route
through sheltered channels
between coastal islands

Kjölen Mountains
"The Keel"

Åland

SWEDEN

ESTONIA

NORWAY

Uppsala

Uppland
Mälaren

Stockholm

♦ its good land and many navigable
waterways made this the most
densely populated area of
Viking-age Sweden

Svealand

Sogne Fjord
Hordaland
Bergen
Hardånger Fjord

Oslo

Vänern

Baltic Sea

Vättern

Gotland

LATVIA

♦ its commanding position in
the Baltic made Gotland a
major centre of Viking trade

Rogaland

Vestfold

Götaland

Southern
Uplands

Stavanger

Göteborg

Öland

LITHUANIA

♦ hill, forest and lake
region: natural frontier
between Danes and
Swedes

Skagerrak

Kattegat

Limfjord
Ålborg

Skåne

Copenhagen

Bornholm

Jutland
Århus

Malmö

DENMARK

Sjælland

North
Sea

♦ sheltered Limfjord,
main sailing route between
North Sea and Baltic
in Viking times

Kiel

POLAND

GERMANY

**Climate and arable land in
Scandinavia**

land over 200 metres

land over 500 metres

land over 1000 metres

arable soil

average January temperature
0¡C (eastern limit)

average July temperature
15¡C (northern limit)

1000mm mean annual rainfall
(eastern limit)

Scandinavia Before the Vikings

The hallmarks of Viking society—trade, seaborne raids and a warrior elite—have their roots in the earlier Iron Age.

Scandinavia was first settled by bands of hunter-gatherers moving north in the wake of retreating ice sheets about 8000 years ago. Farming was practised in southern Scandinavia by 4000 BC, bronze-working by 2000 BC and iron-working by 500 BC. Little is known about Scandinavia in the Early Iron Age (*c.* 500 BC–AD 1): few settlements have been discovered and the most important finds are the superbly preserved bodies of human sacrificial victims which are sometimes found in Danish peat bogs. During the Roman Iron Age (*c.* AD 1–400) chiefly dwellings, cult centres, richly furnished warrior burials and votive hoards of weapons appear in southern Scandinavia. These point to the emergence of a warrior aristocracy and the beginnings of political centralization. The impetus for this was probably competition to control the wealth generated by contacts with the Roman Empire.

The votive offerings of a ship and weapons from Hjortspring (*c.* 350 BC) suggests that sea-raiding was already common in Scandinavia during the Early Iron Age. The Heruls (from Jutland) raided Frisia in AD 287 and Spain in *c.* 455 and *c.* 460, while the Danes are known to have raided Frisia in *c.* 528 and *c.* 570. The migrations of the Jutes and Angles from Jutland to Britain in the 5th century are also unlikely to have been entirely peaceful. Scandinavia largely escaped the dislocation suffered in the rest of Europe during the Migration Period (*c.* 400–600). Fortified local power centres, such as Eketorp on Öland, and the impressive burial mounds at Gamla Uppsala point to the emergence of well-organized chiefdoms. The final period of the Scandinavian Iron Age before the Viking Age was the Vendel period or Late Germanic Iron Age (*c.* 600–800). A rampart—the Danevirke—was built to protect Denmark from the south, and lavish ship burials were made—evidence that Scandinavia's first regional kingdoms had developed.

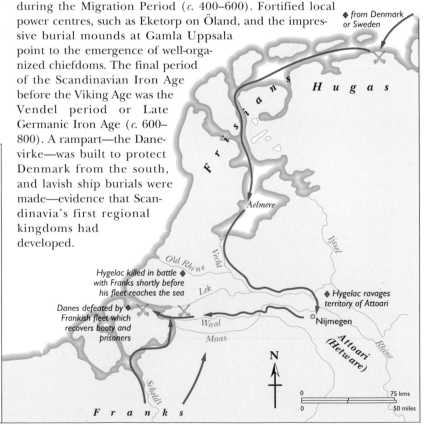

I/Hygelac's raid, 528

One of the earliest recorded Scandinavian pirate raids on western Europe was by Hygelac, a king of the Danes or the Geats (i.e. Götar), c. AD 528. The raiders were defeated by the Franks on the lower Rhine, but they created a lasting impression as the raid is recorded in four independent literary sources including Gregory of Tours's 6th-century history of the Franks and the 8th-century Anglo-Saxon epic poem Beowulf.

- ~~~ 6th-century coastline
- ➤ Danes
- ➤ Franks
- ✕ battle

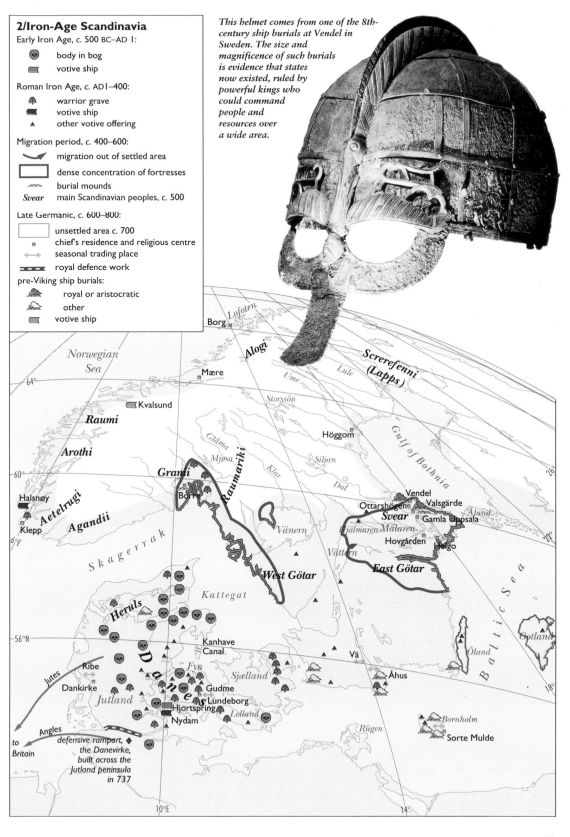

2/Iron-Age Scandinavia

Early Iron Age, c. 500 BC–AD 1:

body in bog

votive ship

Roman Iron Age, c. AD 1–400:

warrior grave

votive ship

other votive offering

Migration period, c. 400–600:

migration out of settled area

dense concentration of fortresses

burial mounds

Svear   main Scandinavian peoples, c. 500

Late Germanic, c. 600–800:

unsettled area c. 700

chief's residence and religious centre

seasonal trading place

royal defence work

pre-Viking ship burials:

royal or aristocratic

other

votive ship

This helmet comes from one of the 8th-century ship burials at Vendel in Sweden. The size and magnificence of such burials is evidence that states now existed, ruled by powerful kings who could command people and resources over a wide area.

Norwegian Sea

Borg

Lofoten

Alogi

Screrefenni (Lapps)

Mære

Ume

Lule

64°

Raumi

Kvalsund

Storsjön

Höggom

Arothi

Gläma

Mjøsa

Grami

Siljan

Klar

60°

Borre

Raumariki

Dal

Vendel

Ottarshögen

Valsgärde

Halsnøy

Åland

Gamla Uppsala

Aetelrugi

Svear

Klepp

Agandii

Vänern

Hjälmaren Mälaren

Hovgården

Helgö

6°

Skagerrak

Vättern

East Götar

West Götar

Gotland

Baltic Sea

Heruls

Kattegat

56°N

Öland

Kanhave

Canal

Vä

Ribe

Fyn

Åhus

Jutes

Sjælland

Dankirke

Gudme

Jutland

Lundeborg

Daneir

Hjortspring

Lolland

Nydam

Angles

Rügen

Bornholm

to

Britain

defensive rampart,

the Danevirke,

built across the

Jutland peninsula

in 737

Sorte Mulde

10°E

14°

Pagan Religion and Burial Customs

Most Vikings were pagans, and the old gods Thor, Odin and Freyr lived on in Scandinavia long after much of Europe was Christian.

Unlike Christianity, Scandinavian paganism did not have a systematic theology and lacked absolute concepts of good and evil or of the afterlife. Religion was a matter of the correct performance and observance of sacrifices, rituals and festivals, rather than of personal spirituality. There was no full-time priesthood; it was usually the king or local chieftains who had the responsibility for ensuring that festivals were observed. A cycle of cosmological myths told of the creation of the world and of its ultimate destruction. Vikings believed that all things were subject to fate, including the gods who would perish at Ragnarök, the final cataclysm that would destroy the world.

As in other polytheistic religions, the Viking gods ruled over different aspects of human life. The most important were Odin, Thor and Freyr. Odin was a rather sinister deity who, with his brothers, had created the human race and gave man the knowledge of poetry and of writing in runes. Odin was the god of wisdom, power, war and poetry: he was a sorcerer and could deprive men of their wits and exercise his power of life and death in wildly unpredictable ways. Odin's attributes made him the god of kings, chieftains, warriors and poets: both the Danish royal family and the Earls of Hlaðir claimed descent from him. The most popular god among the peasantry was Thor, the god of physical strength, thunder and lightning, wind, rain, good weather and crops. Using his mighty hammer Mjöllnir, Thor defended the world against the destructive power of the giants. Unlike Odin, Thor was a straightforward, reliable god, but he was none too bright and the myths concerning his deeds often highlight in a humorous way the limitations of brute strength. Pendants fashioned in the sign of the hammer were often worn by Thor's devotees.

Freyr was the god of wealth, health and fertility: he was portrayed with an erect phallus. Offerings were made to Freyr at weddings. The Swedish Yngling dynasty traced its ancestry to a union between Freyr and Gerd, a giant woman. Freyr had a sister and female counterpart Freyja, who gave luck in love and represented sensuality. Freyja was the leader of the *dísir*, a race of female demigods who presided over fertility in nature and in humans. The god Loki was a cunning, witty mischief-maker, whose schemes were always getting the gods and himself into trouble. Though he was not an unambiguously evil figure like Satan, Loki was capable of great wickedness and treachery, and the Vikings believed that his scheming would lead in the end to Ragnarök.

The Vikings had rather vague ideas about the afterlife. The souls of heroic warriors who had died in battle were taken by the Valkyries—female demigods—to feast and fight in Odin's home, Valhalla, the hall of the slain, until the time came for them to march out to fight side by side with the gods against the giants at Ragnarök. Freyja too might claim a share of the warriors' souls, as well as at least some women's. Others went to the dismal twilight world of Hel. It was also believed that the dead could live on in the

Above: Thor goes fishing for the world serpent. In his right hand he wields his hammer Mjöllnir, ready to stun the beast. This scene appears on a runestone from the church at Altuna in Sweden, testimony to the long coexistence of Christianity and paganism in much of Scandinavia.

Above right: a warrior rides into Valhalla on Odin's eight-legged horse Sleipnir and is welcomed by a Valkyrie. The scene appears on an 8th-century stone carving from the island of Gotland.

Above: high-ranking Scandinavians were often buried in ships, surrounded by grave goods. Here, at the Viking cemetery at Lindholm Høje in Denmark, stones were placed around the grave to form the outline of a ship.

Paganism in Scandinavia, c.800–1000

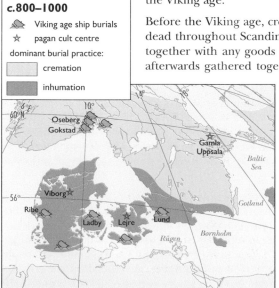

Viking age ship burials

★   pagan cult centre

dominant burial practice:

cremation

inhumation

grave. The common practice of placing everyday objects, weapons, tools and even horses, wagons and ships in graves is probably a sign that people believed that the afterlife would resemble this life, and that somehow these objects would be useful to the dead. However, in some cases, such as the rich ship burials at Oseberg and Gokstad, the grave goods may have been intended more to impress the living with the wealth and status of the deceased's family than to help the dead. Whatever the beliefs that lay behind it, the practice of furnishing graves in this way has provided archaeologists with a major source of information about Scandinavian society in the Viking age.

Before the Viking age, cremation was the normal method of disposal of the dead throughout Scandinavia. The dead were cremated in everyday clothes together with any goods that were to accompany them. The remains were afterwards gathered together and placed in an pottery urn and buried or scattered on the ground. The grave could be marked by a mound or pile of stones or, as at Lindholm Høje, by ship-shaped settings of stones. Early in the Viking age inhumation began to be practiced in Denmark, Gotland and Birka. The richer inhumations were of the "chamber grave" type, where the body was laid fully clothed in a timber-lined pit surrounded by grave goods and sometimes horses or human sacrifices. The common people would be more likely to be buried in a simple wooden coffin or birch-bark shroud. With the spread of Christianity, inhumation, without grave goods, became the normal burial practice across Scandinavia by around 1000.

II: Scandinavia in the Viking Age

The Viking age was a period of prosperity in Scandinavia. The influx of wealth from trading and raiding boosted the economy. The population was rising; new villages were founded and the area under cultivation increased. Scandinavia's first towns developed and the medieval kingdoms of Denmark, Norway and Sweden emerged.

With the start of Viking raids in the last decade of the 8th century, western Europeans, not surprisingly, began to take a greater interest in Scandinavia than they had before, and contemporary literary evidence becomes more plentiful. Western European writers understandably tended to concentrate on what the Vikings were getting up to abroad, however, and though there are numerous scattered references to events in Scandinavia, there are long periods for which they give no evidence at all. These accounts can be supplemented by the works of later Scandinavian historians such as the 12th-century Dane Saxo Grammaticus and the 13th-century authors of the Icelandic sagas. Though vivid and realistic in style, these later works are based largely on orally transmitted historical traditions and contain unreliable and even fictionalized material, so they have to be used with some caution. The Scandinavians themselves were not fully literate in the Viking age, but runes (which had come into use in the Roman Iron Age) were used for charms and for memorial inscriptions, some of which include valuable historical information. Despite the limitations of the sources, it is fair to say that the Viking age marks the end of Scandinavian prehistory.

The Free and the Unfree

Scandinavian society in the Viking age was divided into the free and the unfree. Of the unfree—the slaves—we know very little, but their treatment probably varied greatly according to their skill and abilities, and many were freed as a reward for good service. The free shared the right to bear arms, to speak at the local assembly (the allthing) and to the protection of the law. Though most freemen were tenant or freehold farmers, Scandinavian society was not egalitarian, and the free class included a great range of wealth and status, from the landless labourer to the aristocracy. This inequality was reflected in the scale of fines laid down by law to compound a homicide: the more wealthy and influential the victim, the higher the fine that had to be paid to his family by the guilty party. As legal judgements had to be enforced by the individuals concerned, this also put poorer freemen at a disadvantage unless they had a powerful lord to force the guilty party to comply. Though hierarchical, society was not static, and the Viking age offered the ambitious and the able many opportunities to increase their wealth and raise their status by joining pirate or trading expeditions overseas or by entering royal service.

The aristocracy exercised considerable power locally, even down to resiting and replanning whole villages. The aristocracy played a leading role at the local assembly, where they would arbitrate in legal disputes, and also at the more important regional assemblies (*things*) where major issues were discussed. The aristocracy's power and influence was based on landownership, and by offering protection to less powerful men in return for their political support. The highest of the aristocracy bore the title *jarl* (English "earl"), which probably originally meant simply "prominent man". The most power-ful jarls, such as those of Hlaðir in Trondelag or of Orkney, were consider-able rulers in their own right, exercising virtually royal powers over wide ter-ritories. The aristocracy played an important role as war leaders, organizing local defences and raising contingents of troops for the royal army. Some chieftains led Viking raids and the most successful, like the Dane Thorkell the Tall at the end of the 10th century, built up such large armed followings that they became potential rivals to the king. The independence of the aris-tocracy was challenged in the Viking age by the growth of royal power which sought to exercise direct authority at a local level, rather than having to work through the intermediary of the local chieftains.

Struggles for Power

By the beginning of the Viking age, monarchy was already the dominant force in society. Though the power of the monarchy was limited to some extent by the need for the king to consult the assemblies before taking major decisions, the king usually got his own way. For example, when St Anskar asked King Olaf of the Svear for permission to preach in 850, the king told him that he would have to seek the approval of the assembly. The proposal initially aroused opposition but Olaf, who favoured Christianity, was able to manipulate proceedings to persuade the assembly to agree. Another theoretical limitation on the power of the monarchy was that the king had to be accepted by the more important assemblies. In practice this was usually a formality and, if necessary, the assemblies could be overawed by an impressive show of force, as Olaf Tryggvason did with the Norwegian assemblies in 995.

Below: Reconstructions of Viking-age trading ships under sail in Roskilde Fjord, Denmark. The growth of trade in Viking-age Scandinavia led to the development of a variety of specialist merchant ships: right, a small coaster and left, a deep-sea trader or knarr. Unlike warships, merchants relied on their sails for propulsion.

The king's income came from landownership, tolls on trade, tribute and plunder from war. Royal administration was rudimentary and was performed by members of the king's retinue, the *hirð*, probably appointed on an ad hoc basis for a specific task. Kings moved constantly from estate to estate: they had favoured residences but the Viking kingdoms did not have permanent administrative capitals. Viking kings were primarily rulers of men rather than rulers of territory. Though usually the two went together, it was not always necessary to have a kingdom to be recognized as a king: many of the 9th-century Viking leaders were kings who, apparently, possessed no lands.

Right: *This silver ring from Hornelund in Denmark was made in the 10th century, a fine example of Viking craftmanship in precious metals.*

The rules governing royal succession were that a king had to be descended from a king on either his father's or his mother's side. A king might usually be succeeded by one of his sons, but any male member of the royal dynasty was eligible. This meant that there could be many potential claimants for the throne, and succession disputes were common. Joint kings were a common expedient when rival claimants who had equal support were prepared to compromise, but disputed successions often led to civil wars. The losers in these civil wars, if they survived, went into exile to lick their wounds. All was not lost for exiles of royal blood: they might persuade the ruler of a neighbouring kingdom to provide them with military support to renew the struggle or they might use the prestige that came from possessing royal blood to raise a warrior band and go plundering. With luck, an exile might acquire wealth, fame and a mighty following of warriors with which to try once again to win power at home or a kingdom overseas. Returning exiles were a major destabilizing influence in the Viking kingdoms and a constant headache for established kings.

Denmark

The Viking kingdom we know most about in this period is Denmark. By around 800 the Danes had already created a kingdom which included all of modern Denmark, part of Germany and the provinces of Skåne and Halland which are now in Sweden. The Danish kings also seem to have exercised some form of dominion over the Vestfold region of Norway. In the early Middle Ages Skåne and Halland formed the Danes' "mark", or border, which gave its name to the whole country.

The main preoccupation of the Danish kings at the beginning of the Viking period was the threat (real or imagined) of Frankish expansionism. Godfred, the first Danish king about whom we know much more than his name, pursued an aggressive policy towards the Franks, attacking their Slav allies in 808 and leading a large fleet to ravage Frisia in 810. Godfred also rebuilt and extended the Danevirke rampart in 808, to protect Jutland from Frankish invasion. After Godfred was murdered in 810, his nephew Hemming became king and Godfred's sons fled into exile. Two years later Hemming died, and the crown was fought over by Sigfred, another nephew of Godfred, and Anulo, a nephew of an earlier king. Sigfred and Anulo were both killed in the battle which followed, but Anulo's party was victorious and chose his brothers Harald Klak and Reginfred as joint kings. In 813 the sons of Godfred returned and drove Harald and Reginfred into exile where they recruited an army and tried, but failed, to win their throne back the following year. Reginfred was killed and Harald went into exile in Francia. When Godfred's sons fell out among themselves in 819, Harald returned and became joint king with one faction of the Godfred sons but was driven out again in 827. By the 830s only one of Godfred's sons, Horik, survived. He was to hold onto his power until 853 when he was overthrown by a rebellion within his own family.

Little is known about Denmark for the next century. The kingdom was frequently divided and for some time around 900 at least part of it was ruled by a Swedish dynasty. Around the mid 10th century, Gorm the Old (d. 958) founded a new, and soon to be illustrious, dynasty. Gorm's son, Harald Bluetooth united Denmark and built a series of fortresses across the kingdom to secure his direct authority in all parts of the country. Denmark was under pressure from the Germans in the 10th century; in 974 they occupied Hedeby, but were driven out seven years later by Harald. In 987 Harald was deposed by his son Svein Forkbeard.

Viking raiding had begun to revive in the late 10th century, and successful Viking leaders like Olaf Tryggvason and Thorkell the Tall rivalled Svein in prestige and wealth. Svein bolstered his own position by leading his own highly successful raids against England. At first Svein was content to milk England for Danegeld, but as English resistance crumbled he conquered the country in 1013, only to die a few months later.

Norway

At the beginning of the Viking period Norway was divided up into something like a dozen chiefdoms and petty kingdoms, and local identities were still very strong. The Vestfold was probably the most politically advanced area of the country in the 8th century, but by around 800 this region was under Danish control. Danish influence declined as a result of the damaging succession disputes of the 9th century, and shortly before 900 the king of Vestfold, Harald Finehair, succeeded in winning control of much of Norway at the battle of Hafrsfjord. For this achievement Harald is traditionally credited with being the founder of the Norwegian kingdom. He and his successors, however, faced the continuing opposition of the powerful jarls of Hlaðir. Harald reigned for some 50 years, and was succeeded around 930 by his son Erik Bloodaxe. Erik was soon driven off the throne by his younger brother Hakon the Good, and went into exile to earn a fearsome reputation as a Viking leader and to become, for two short periods between 948 and 954, King of York. Hakon was killed some time around 960 by Erik Bloodaxe's son Harald Greycloak, who then became king. Harald spent much of his reign trying unsuccessfully to gain control of the Trondelag, and was eventually killed around 970 fighting against an alliance of Jarl Hakon of Hlaðir and Svein Forkbeard. The allies restored Norway to Danish control—if the jarls of Hlaðir had to submit to a king, they preferred to do so to a distant rather than a near one.

Hakon remained the most powerful man in Norway until 995, when Olaf Tryggvason, a grandson of Harald Finehair who had won much fame and wealth as a Viking leader, invaded, put Hakon to flight and established himself as king over the whole country. Olaf ruled only five years before being killed at Svöld (location unknown) in battle against an alliance between Svein Forkbeard and Jarl Erik of Hlaðir. Svein and Erik divided control of the country between them, but Norway had been united and it would be again before long.

Sweden

Sweden is the Scandinavian country we know least about in this period. There were two main peoples, the Svear, from whom Sweden takes its name, in the region around Lake Mälaren, and the Götar around Lakes Vänern and Vättern. Very little is known about the Götar, and they are not mentioned in primary sources as being involved in Viking raiding (though that might only be the result of confusion over identities). The names of a few Svear kings are known from the 9th century, but the extent of their authority is not known with any precision. However, by around 890 the Svear kingdom probably included most of central Sweden and the islands of Gotland and Öland. The relationship between the Svear and Götar appears to have been close, and some Svear kings were actually of Götar origin. The first king known for certain to have ruled both the Svear and the Götar was Olof Skötkonung (ruled c. 995–1020), but the unification of the two peoples in a single kingdom was not complete until the 12th century.

From Pagan to Christian

The period between 800 and1000 saw the beginning of the Christianization of Scandinavia. The Vikings came into contact with Christianity through preaching missions like St Anskar's, which began in the 820s, and also through their activities in the Christian lands. Many early conversions may have been motived by practical rather than spiritual concerns. The first Viking king to be baptized, Harald Klak in 826, probably did so to win the support of Emperor Louis the Pious against his rivals at home. Christian rulers such as Alfred the Great often made baptism a condition of peace treaties. Some Vikings were baptized several times in this way without ever truly accepting Christianity. The Annals of St Bertin record that after a Frankish abbot had baptized a group of Vikings in 876 "he bestowed gifts on them and sent them back to their own people, but afterwards, like typical Northmen, they lived according to the pagan custom just as before." Despite such setbacks, Christianity was well established among the Viking settlers overseas by 900. Christianity was tolerated in Scandinavia from the early 9th century, and there were churches in Hedeby, Ribe and Birka by the 850s. The Vikings seem to have readily accepted Christ as a god to be invoked along with the traditional Norse gods, but it took far longer for the

Christian god to be accepted as the sole god. An Icelander, Helgi the Lean, said that he was a Christian "but invoked Thor in matters of seafaring and dire necessity." The real breakthrough for Christianity came only in the later 10th century, when kings like Harald Bluetooth and Olaf Tryggvason converted. While no doubt sincere enough converts, these kings recognized the potential of Christian doctrines and church organization as a means of strengthening the monarchy and promoting the unity of their kingdoms.

Right: Thor was the most popular of the Norse gods, and his hammer symbol was often worn to invoke his protection. This 10th-century amulet was found in Iceland; its design has been strongly influenced by the Christian crucifix.

From Chiefdoms to Kingdoms

The kings of Denmark emerged as the most powerful force in Scandinavia as chiefdoms gave way to organized states.

Above: Harald Bluetooth's rune stone in the Danish royal cemetery at Jelling would originally have been brightly painted. It is inscribed: "King Harald commanded these memorials made to Gorm his father and Thyre his mother, that Harald who won for himself all Denmark and Norway and made the Danes Christian." The newly baptized king had the pagan great beast and serpent engraved on this side of the stone, and the figure of Christ on the other.

When Scandinavia emerged from its prehistoric period at the end of the 8th century, the Danes were politically the most advanced of the Scandinavian peoples. The kings of Denmark dominated an area far larger than modern Denmark; their overlordship was recognized over much of what is now southern Sweden and as far north as Vestfold in Norway. Kings were chosen from a single royal family, but any member of that family could aspire to the kingship. As a result, succession disputes were common. Unsuccessful claimants often went into exile to pursue a career as Viking leaders in order to win wealth and reputation to make a fresh bid for the throne. This destabilized the Danish monarchy, and its authority collapsed in the second half of the 9th century.

Shortly before 900 Harald Finehair (d. *c.*930), a king or chieftain in Vest-fold, exploited the collapse of Danish power to make himself master of most of southern Norway. Harald is traditionally seen as the founder of the Norwegian kingdom, though his control over the powerful Jarls of Hlaðir in the Trondelag remained weak. By the mid-10th century Danish power was reviving under King Gorm (d. 958) and his son Harald Bluetooth (958–87) re-established Danish control over Norway. Harald was baptized in 965 and became the first Scandinavian king actively to promote Christianity. Harald's successor Svein Forkbeard increased the wealth and authority of the monarchy by leading a series of well organized and successful raids on England, culminating in his conquest of the country in 1013. By leading the raids himself, Svein largely prevented any other Viking getting enough wealth and prestige to challenge his throne, though in 995 a Norwegian Viking, Olaf Tryggvason, did temporarily establish himself as king of Norway. He lost his kingdom and his life at the Battle of Svöld in 1000.

The history of Sweden in this period is less well known. The Svear and the neighbouring Götar people appear to have had a close relationship, and by 975 Olof Skötkonung was described as king of the Svear and Götar. The two peoples were not securely united until the 12th century, however. The Svear kings also collected tribute from Finnish areas east of the Baltic. Danish influence was not as strong as in Norway, but Olof, whose nickname "Skötkonung" means tributary king, acknowledged Svein as overlord.

2/The round fort at Fyrkat

This is one of four round forts in Denmark which were probably built around 980 by Harald Bluetooth. They all follow a standard design, suggesting that they were planned by a central authority with power over considerable amounts of labour and resources. Earlier Danish kings had exercised power indirectly through the chieftains; by building and garrisoning these forts (known as Trelleborg-type round forts), Harald could control his kingdom directly.

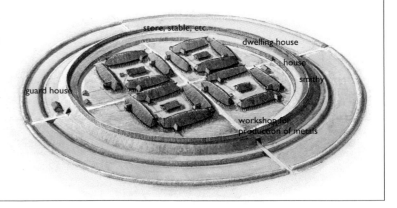

store, stable, etc.

dwelling house

house

smithy

guard house

workshop for production of metals

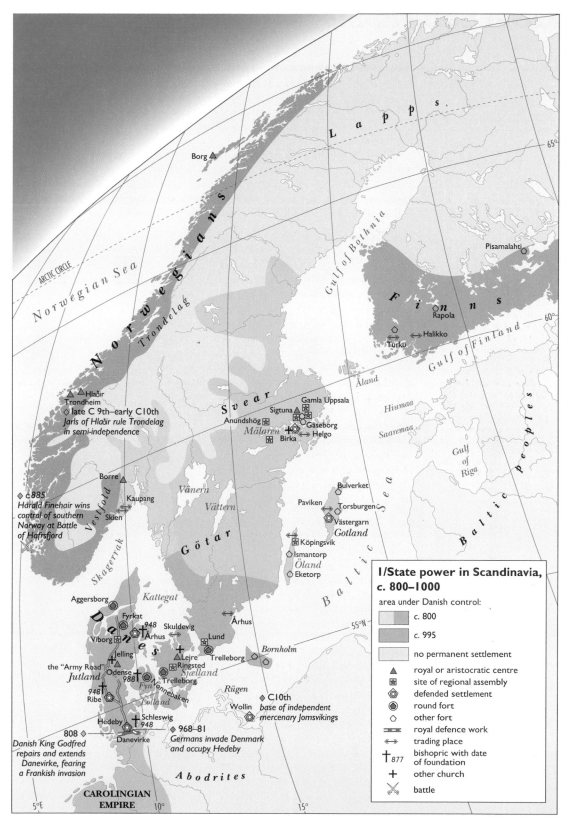

Borg

Lapps

ARCTIC CIRCLE

Norwegian Sea

65°

Gulf of Bothnia

Pisamalahti

F i n n s

Rapola

60°

Halikko

Turku

Gulf of Finland

Hlaðir
Trondheim
◇ late C 9th–early C10th
*Jarls of Hlaðir rule Trondelag
in semi-independence*

S v e a r

Sigtuna Gamla Uppsala

Anundshög

Mälaren Gäseborg

Birka Helgo

Åland

Hiumaa

Saaremaa

*Gulf
of
Riga*

Borre

◇ c.885
*Harald Finehair wins
control of southern
Norway at Battle
of Hafrsfjord*

Kaupang

Skien

Vänern

Vättern

Vestfold

Bulverket

Paviken Torsburgen

Västergarn

Gotland

Köpingsvik

Ismantorp

Öland
Eketorp

G ö t a r

Skagerrak

Baltic peoples

Baltic Sea

Aggersborg

Kattegat

Fyrkat

948 Skuldevig

Viborg Århus

Árhus

Lund

Jelling

the "Army Road"

Odense

Jutland

988

Lejre

Ringsted

Trelleborg

Fyn Tønnebaken

Lolland

Trelleborg

Bornholm

Rügen

Wollin

◇ C10th
*base of independent
mercenary Jomsvikings*

948
Ribe

Hedeby

Schleswig
948

968–81
*Germans invade Denmark
and occupy Hedeby*

Danevirke

808 ◇
*Danish King Godfred
repairs and extends
Danevirke, fearing
a Frankish invasion*

A b o d r i t e s

**CAROLINGIAN
EMPIRE**

D a n e s

Sjælland

**I/State power in Scandinavia,
c. 800–1000**

area under Danish control:

	c. 800
	c. 995
	no permanent settlement

▲ royal or aristocratic centre

⊞ site of regional assembly

◉ defended settlement

◉ round fort

◇ other fort

⟷ royal defence work

↔ trading place

✝877 bishopric with date
of foundation

✚ other church

⚔ battle

5°E   10°   15°

55°N

Rural Settlement

Most Scandinavians of the Viking age lived peacefully by agriculture, rearing animals and growing crops in small villages.

"Ohthere was among the foremost men of [Halogaland]; yet he did not have more than 20 head of cattle, and 20 sheep, and 20 pigs; and the little that he ploughed, he ploughed by horses."

Ohthere's voyage to the White Sea, c. 890

The main farming activity in all the settled parts of Scandinavia—including Halogaland, well beyond the Arctic Circle—was animal husbandry; cattle, pigs, sheep and goats were all reared by the Vikings. In Denmark and southern Sweden, arable farming was also important; the main crops were barley, rye, oats, peas, beans and cabbage. Denmark may even have produced surplus grain. In Arctic Norway and the marginal upland areas of Norway and Sweden, hunting and fishing made a significant contribution to the diet as well as providing valuable trade goods.

In Denmark small villages were the normal form of settlement. These villages seem to have shifted their sites slightly every hundred years or so, and only settled down onto permananent sites after the end of the Viking age. There are few large areas of fertile land in Norway, and the broken nature of the terrain led to a dispersed settlement pattern with isolated farms on small pockets of cultivable land. In Sweden too, settlement was dispersed, but in the fertile areas of Västergötland and Uppland, villages were beginning to appear by the end of the Viking age as a result of the subdivision of existing farms. The population of Scandinavia was rising during the Viking age, and the period saw an expansion of the area under cultivation and the creation of new settlements where enough suitable land could be claimed in between established settlements.

The most typical Viking-age farm building was the long house, which accommodated both people and animals under one roof. Farms had many outbuildings for use as workshops or storage. A common type of smaller building was the sunken-floored hut, which was half buried in the ground. These buildings were well insulated and may have been used for storing products which needed to be kept cool. Building techniques reflected the local environment. In much of Norway and Sweden, where timber was plentiful, buildings had solid wooden walls and roofs made of a layer of waterproof birch bark covered with insulating turf. In less forested areas such as Jutland, timber-framed buildings were walled with clay-plastered wattle and roofed with thatch. In treeless areas such as Iceland, turf and stone were used as much as possible.

Above: the wooden spade was one of the standard agricultural implements of the Viking world. This 8th-century example is made of oak, and has seen considerable wear. It was found in one of the wells at Vorbasse.

Vorbasse

Vorbasse: a Viking farming village

Vorbasse in Jutland is the only complete Viking farming village to have been excavated. The site has a complex history of occupation lasting from around 100 BC to AD 1100, when the village moved to its present location about 750m to the south. In the period from 700–1000 there were six farms in the village, all of roughly the same size. The main occupation was stock rearing —the farms had about 20 cows each—but grain was also grown. The village must have produced a surplus of food which could be traded for the necessities it could not provide for itself: good building timber, iron, whetstones and soapstone pots from Norway, and good quality pottery and lava quernstones from the Rhineland.

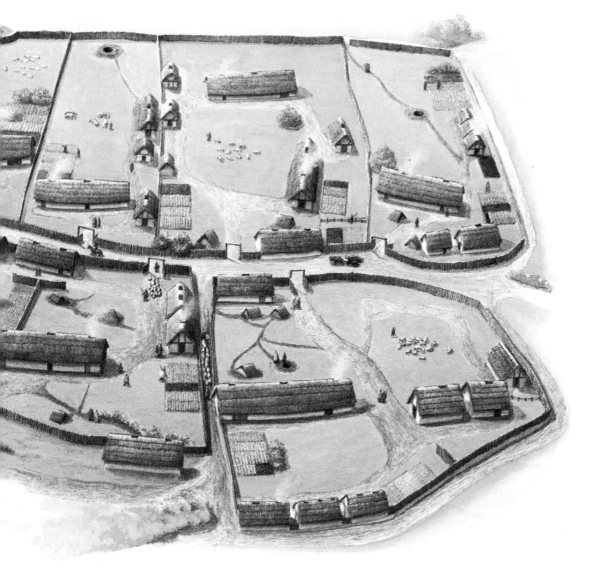

Trade and Trade Routes

Alongside raiding and settlement, Vikings operated a far-flung trade network from Greenland to Central Asia.

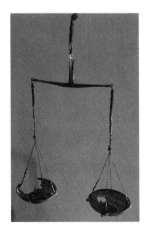

Above: *in Viking transactions, silver was valued by weight. This pair of balance scales from Viking Dublin dates from the 9th century and would have been used for weighing coins or hacksilver.*

Scandinavian trade with the rest of Europe increased in the 8th century, and probably encouraged the Viking expansion. Scandinavians on trading voyages would have become aware of the unguarded riches of western Europe, while the growing fur trade provided the incentive for the Swedes to establish themselves in northern Russia. Some Scandinavians made a living exclusively as merchants, but most were part-timers who also engaged in farming, crafts or even piracy. The most valuable goods were initially acquired as plunder or tribute. Huge amounts of silver, paid as Danegeld, came from England and Francia; furs and slaves were extorted as tribute from the Finns, Lapps and Slavs and then traded for silver with the Arabs. Wealth flooded into Scandinavia during the 9th and 10th centuries; on the Baltic island of Gotland alone, 40,000 Arabic, 38,000 Frankish and 21,000 Anglo-Saxon silver coins have been found in hoards from this period.

Most trade was short-distance, conducted by farmer-merchants to and from dozens of small ports around the Scandinavian coasts. A smaller number of international trading places attracted merchants from England, Frisia, Germany and occasionally even as far afield as the Caliphate of Baghdad. Most of these centres began as seasonal meeting places where craftsmen set up temporary workshops and merchants could trade by barter or for silver. Successful centres, like Hedeby and Ribe, developed into Scandinavia's first towns. Kings sought to encourage and control trade by protecting merchants from piracy in exchange for tolls and taxes. In this way, trade aided the growth of royal power in Scandinavia.

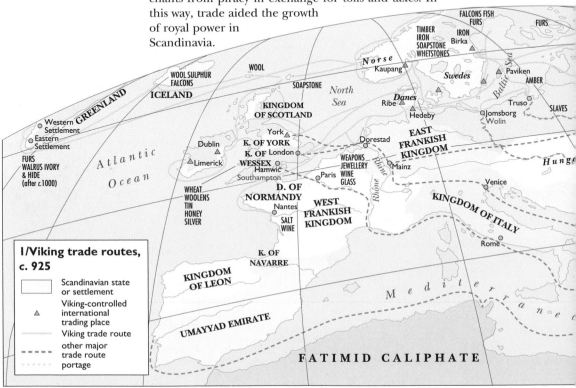

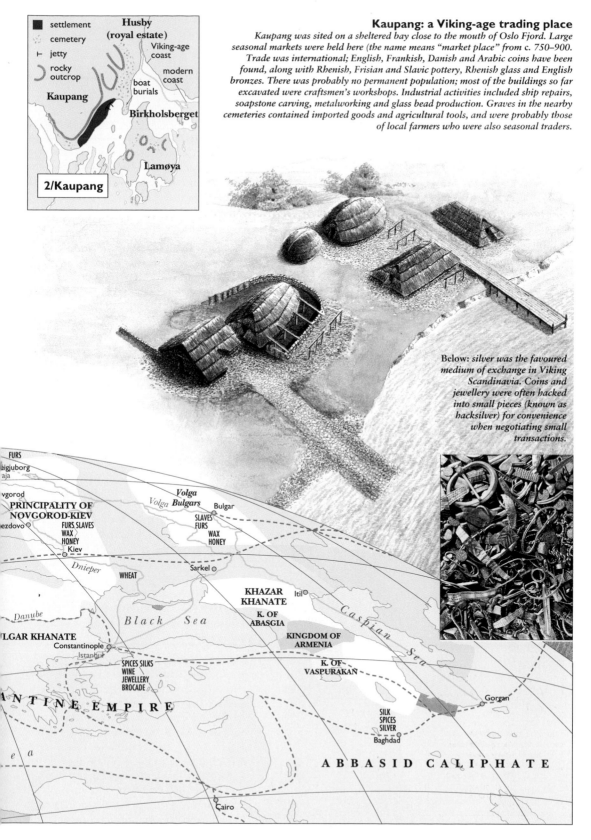

Kaupang: a Viking-age trading place

Kaupang was sited on a sheltered bay close to the mouth of Oslo Fjord. Large seasonal markets were held here (the name means "market place" from c. 750–900. Trade was international; English, Frankish, Danish and Arabic coins have been found, along with Rhenish, Frisian and Slavic pottery, Rhenish glass and English bronzes. There was probably no permanent population; most of the buildings so far excavated were craftsmen's workshops. Industrial activities included ship repairs, soapstone carving, metalworking and glass bead production. Graves in the nearby cemeteries contained imported goods and agricultural tools, and were probably those of local farmers who were also seasonal traders.

Map key (2/Kaupang)

- ■ settlement
- ⋮ cemetery
- ⊢ jetty
- 〰 rocky outcrop

Husby (royal estate)
Viking-age coast
modern coast
boat burials
Kaupang
Birkholsberget
Lamøya

2/Kaupang

Below: silver was the favoured medium of exchange in Viking Scandinavia. Coins and jewellery were often hacked into small pieces (known as hacksilver) for convenience when negotiating small transactions.

FURS
eigjuborg
aja
vgorod
PRINCIPALITY OF NOVGOROD-KIEV
ezdovo
FURS SLAVES
WAX
HONEY
Kiev
Volga
Volga **Bulgars**
Bulgar
SLAVES
FURS
WAX
HONEY
Dnieper
WHEAT
Sarkel
KHAZAR KHANATE
Itil
K. OF ABASGIA
Danube
Black Sea
KINGDOM OF ARMENIA
Caspian Sea
LGAR KHANATE
Constantinople
Istanbul
SPICES SILKS
WINE
JEWELLERY
BROCADE
K. OF VASPURAKAN
Gorgan
NTINE EMPIRE
SILK
SPICES
SILVER
Baghdad
e a
ABBASID CALIPHATE
Cairo

Ships and Seafaring

Without seaworthy sailing ships, the Viking expansion would have been impossible. Their importance is demonstrated in art, poetry, religion and burial practices.

"The winter after King Olaf came from Halogaland, he had a great vessel built at Ladehammer, which was larger than any ship in the country… Thorberg Skafhogg was… the master builder of the ship; but there were many others besides—some to fell wood, some to shape it, some to make nails, some to carry timber; and all that was used was of the best."

King Olaf Tryggvason's Saga

Viking ships were built using the clinker or lapstrake technique in which the lower edge of each hull plank overlaps the upper edge of the one below it. This technique gave the Viking ships light, flexible hulls which "rode" the waves and had excellent sea-keeping qualities. Viking ships were double-ended, with the bow and the stern built in the same way, and were steered by a side rudder (always on the right, hence starboard). There were many different types of Viking ship, all built to suit a particular purpose or maritime environment.

Typical of a small Viking warship is the 11th-century longship known as Skuldelev 5, found with four other wrecks at Skuldelev near Roskilde in Denmark. The ship was 57 feet (17.5m) long by 8 feet (2.5m) wide, and had a crew of 26 oarsmen. Tests with a replica of the ship have shown that it could reach speeds of over 9 knots under sail and over 5 knots when rowed by a full crew. Even fully loaded it drew only 18 inches (50 cm) of water; it would have been ideally suited to raiding in the shallow waters of the Baltic and the southern North Sea, and could have sailed far inland up rivers. Norwegian longships, such as the Gokstad ship, sailed mostly in deeper Atlantic waters and were broader and had deeper keels than Danish longships. The royal fleets of the late Viking age also included much larger "dragon" ships such as King Olaf Tryggvason's "Long Serpent". At 100 feet (30m) long and needing a crew of over 50 oarsmen, Skuldelev 2 was probably such a ship.

Trade ships, built with cargo carrying capacity in mind, were shorter than longships and had wider, deeper and heavier hulls. Trade ships relied on their sails for propulsion and could be worked by small crews of four to six men: a few oars only were carried for manoeuvring in harbour. The most important type of seagoing trade ship was the sturdy *knarr*, represented by wreck 1 from Skuldelev. This was 54 feet (16.5m) long and had a cargo capacity of 24 tons. The *knarr* was undoubtedly the type of ship which was used for to carry settlers across the North Atlantic to Iceland, Greenland and America (▶ *pages 98–9*). Local trade was carried on in small ships such as Skuldelev 3, which had a cargo capacity of 4 tons.

It is not known exactly how the Vikings navigated their ships. Where it was convenient they hugged the coast, navigating by prominent landmarks ashore: certainly most of the Danish raids on Francia and southern England could have been carried out this way. However, the Vikings, especially the Norwegians, did make considerable open sea voyages on which they could be out of sight of land for several days or longer. Though they lacked the magnetic compass, the

Right: memorial slabs from the Baltic island of Gotland offer the earliest clear evidence of the use of the sail in Scandinavia. This 8th-century stone shows the diagonal stitching in the sail, and the rigging held by the two crew members.

Vikings possessed a simple sun compass which could locate north with tolerable accuracy in clear weather. Viking navigators could also use the stars to judge latitude, a great aid to navigation if the latitude of the destination was known. Navigators would have been heirs to a stock of orally transmitted practical knowledge of sea and weather conditions. The presence of an island over the horizon might be detected by cloud formations or the direction of flight of seabirds; a slackening of the sea in stormy conditions could indicate that the ship had sailed into the lee of an island made invisible by rain or cloud. Despite tricks like these, the Viking seafarer was desperately vulnerable to being blown off course or shipwrecked in bad weather. Sometimes a storm-driven mariner would find his way home to tell of a sighting of a new land, but many more must have been lost without trace.

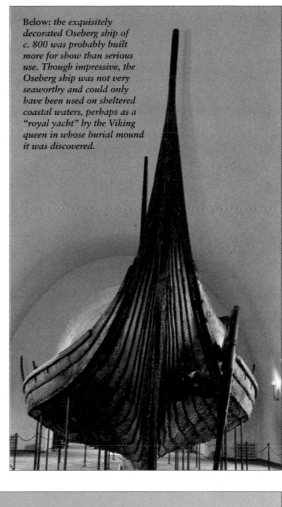

Below: *the exquisitely decorated Oseberg ship of c. 800 was probably built more for show than serious use. Though impressive, the Oseberg ship was not very seaworthy and could only have been used on sheltered coastal waters, perhaps as a "royal yacht" by the Viking queen in whose burial mound it was discovered.*

Below: *fine weather vanes adorned the masts of stems of Viking ships. Originally streamers were attached to the holes in the edge to give an indication of wind speed and strength. The Vikings had few navigational aids and relied on an expert knowledge of landmarks, sea conditions and the positions of the sun and stars to find their way.*

Right: *"Helge Ask", a replica of the Skuldelev 5 ship, a small Danish warship of c. 1000 found in Roskilde Fjord. Swift under sails or oars, even fully laden it has a draught of only 18 inches (50 cm) making it ideally suited for raiding far inland on rivers like the Seine and the Loire.*

Viking Towns

Towns were slow to develop in Viking Age Scandinavia, but by 1000 there were several thriving urban centres.

Scandinavia had no true towns before the Viking age, though there were several seasonal market centres. When towns did spring up, it did not happen spontaneously. Urban development went hand in hand with the growth of royal power, and most towns appear to have been deliberately founded, often on virgin sites, by rulers to encourage, control and profit from trade. By the late 10th century towns were also being founded as administrative and ecclesiastical centres.

The earliest towns in Scandinavia, Ribe, Birka and Hedeby, all date from the late 8th century. The Danish monarchy played an important role in the foundation of Hedeby, and both Ribe and Birka were under close royal control in the early 9th century, suggesting that they too were deliberate royal foundations. Hedeby, the largest of the three towns, had a population of 1000–1500: Ribe and Birka were somewhat smaller. Ribe has survived as a trade, ecclesiastical and administrative centre to the present day, making it Scandinavia's oldest town, but Birka and Hedeby both fell victim to falling sea levels, which made it increasingly difficult for the deeper draughted merchant ships of the 10th century to use them. Birka was abandoned around 970, Hedeby by 1100.

Hedeby, Ribe and Birka remained the only towns in Scandinavia until the 10th century, when Århus was founded, apparently as a craft and manufacturing centre. The pace of urban development increased around 1000: Sigtuna, Trondheim, Oslo, Viborg, Odense, Roskilde and Lund were all founded as administrative or

"[Hedeby] is a large town at the other end of the world sea... The town is not rich in goods... The staple food is fish, since it is so plentiful. It often happens that a newborn infant is tossed into the sea to save raising it. Also ... women may divorce their husbands... Nothing can compare with the dreadful singing of these people, worse even than the barking of dogs." al-Tartushi, an Arab merchant from Spain, *c.* 950

Hedeby
For most of the Viking age Hedeby was Scandinavia's largest town. Though some sort of settlement existed at Hedeby before King Godfred settled a colony of merchants there in 808, it was probably this act that led to Hedeby developing into an international market centre. There was a mint, and the remains of what was probably a toll station have been excavated, but little else is known about the administration of the town. A wide range of manufacturing activities were carried out, including metal, bone, amber and glassworking, pottery and ship repair. In the 10th century Hedeby was provided with substantial defences linking it with the Danevirke rampart but it was sacked by Harald Hardrada in 1050 and by the Wends in 1066. By 1100 Hedeby had been abandoned in favour of nearby Schleswig, probably because Schleswig was easier of access to the deeper draughted merchant ships which were then coming into use.

ecclesiastical centres shortly before or after this date. Urban development was slowest in Sweden, where royal authority developed more slowly than in Denmark and Norway. By 1100 there were still only four towns in Sweden, while in Denmark there were 15 and in Norway there were eight.

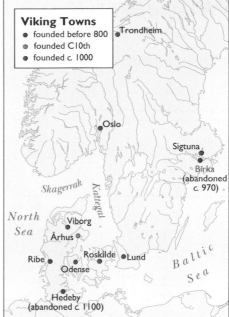

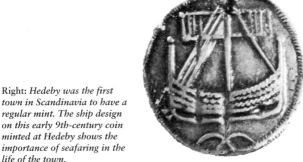

Right: *Hedeby was the first town in Scandinavia to have a regular mint. The ship design on this early 9th-century coin minted at Hedeby shows the importance of seafaring in the life of the town.*

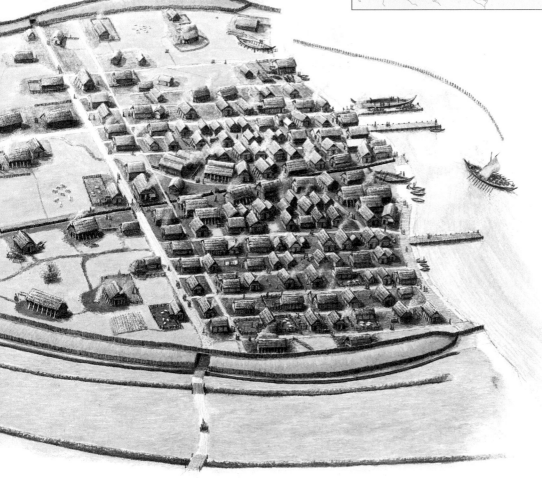

Women in the Viking Age

Scandinavian society was male dominated, but women were far from being chattels: many were strong-minded and had a high status in the community.

"When And the Deep-Minded learned that her son had been killed she realized that she had no further prospects [in Caithness]... So she had a ship built secretly in a forest, and when it was completed she loaded it with valuables and prepared it for a voyage. She took all her surviving kinsfolk... It would be hard to find another example of a woman escaping from such hazards with so much wealth and such a large retinue."
Laxdaela Saga

Above Right: *these bone pins are typical of the cloak fastenings used by Viking-age women for everyday wear. They come from a settlement at the Udall in North Uist in the Outer Hebrides.*

Men and women had clearly defined and separate social roles in Viking-age Scandinavia. Men ploughed, fished, hunted, traded and fought. Most women's lives were more narrowly confined to the home: they milked the cows and churned butter, ground grain and baked bread, spun wool, wove cloth and looked after the children. The grave goods in pagan burials mirror these roles exactly: men were buried with weapons and tools, women with jewellery, needlework and weaving equipment, and other household utensils that would be useful in the afterlife.

Though marriages were usually arranged by negotiations between the prospective husband and the bride's father, the woman's wishes would usually be taken into account. A marriage was regarded as an alliance between equals. The bride normally brought a dowry to the partnership, and the husband paid her a "bride-price"; both remained her property after marriage. Women had the right to a divorce if a marriage proved unworkable, and the marriage contract could stipulate how the joint estate should be divided in such an eventuality. Though they had no role in public life, within the home women exercised great authority over slaves and dependents, and would always be closely involved in major decisions affecting the family. If her husband was away, at war or on business, a wife would have full responsibility for the running of the house and farm in his absence; and if she were widowed she would have to take her husband's place full time. Family honour was of as much concern to women as it was to men. In Icelandic literature at least, they were never slow to urge their menfolk to take revenge for any injury, and it is likely that they took the lead in commemorating the dead. Pagan graves in Denmark suggest that women's status increased with age: some of the most richly furnished burials are of women aged 50 or over, while the quality of grave goods in male burials decreased with the age of the dead man.

Right: two large, intricately-decorated gold disc brooches of the type used by both women and men for fastening cloaks or sleeved coats—a very expensive alternative to the bone pins illustrated on the left.

There is no reliable evidence to suggest that women ever fought as warriors alongside their menfolk, but it is known that at least some of the warriors of the great Viking armies that were active in western Europe in the second half of the 9th century were accompanied by their wives and families. These women would have given useful support to the army, cooking and caring for the wounded. Women, naturally, were much more prominent participants in the Viking settlements in Iceland and Greenland, where their presence was essential from the start. Women in Iceland during the settlement period seem to have enjoyed higher status than those elsewhere in Scandinavia, and strong-minded independent women commonly appear in the sagas. The participation of women in the attempt to settle Vinland is also recorded in the sagas and by finds of spindle whorls at the short-lived Norse settlement at L'Anse-aux-Meadows (▶ *pages 98–9*). There is very little evidence that Scandinavian women accompanied the Rus on their journeys in the east, though finds of typically Scandinavian female artifacts and rare literary references show that there were at least some. Arab sources suggest that most of the Rus found local women; if this is true, it could explain why the Rus were so rapidly assimilated into the native Slav population.

Left: women's clothing of the Viking age can be reconstructed from rags found at Hedeby and Birka. A good-quality outfit would have consisted of a pinafore dress of fine woolen fabric over a long-sleeved, ankle-length linen tunic. A pair of gilt oval brooches would have fastened the dress at the shoulders; gold thread was used to decorate the hem.

Below: a group of everyday household items, including spindle whorls and whetstones from a Viking-age farm at Bryants Gill, Kentmere. Place names suggest that there were many farms in this part of the Lake District during the Viking-age, but Bryants Gill is the only one to have been excavated; the rest are buried under present-day farms. Women's skill with the spindle whorls ensured that Viking-age farms were virtually self-sufficient as far as clothing was concerned.

III: The Viking Raids

The Vikings have become a byword for seaborne terror: violent raiders descending in their longships to plunder monasteries and butcher peaceful communities of men, women and children. But were they really more violent than their Christian contemporaries?

The most hotly debated issues regarding the history of the Vikings are their numbers, and the destructiveness and violence of their raids. Traditionally, the Vikings have been regarded by historians as wantonly cruel, violent and destructive pirate hoards. However, in recent years a new view of the Vikings has gained widespread acceptance. The Vikings, it is argued, were the victims of a bad press: their numbers, violence and destructiveness were greatly exaggerated by monastic chroniclers who were prejudiced against them because of their paganism and their habit of plundering monasteries. Rather than destructive raiders, the Vikings should be regarded primarily as traders, settlers and skilled craftsmen. The level of Viking violence was only worse than that normally prevailing in early medieval Europe in so far as it did not exempt the church.

In fact, these two views of the Vikings are not irreconcilable. Most Viking-age Scandinavians were indeed peaceful farmers, craftsment and traders whose lives were probably rarely touched by violence. However, those Scandinavians who chose warfare or piracy as a profession, that is the warriors who went *i viking* and participated in the plundering expeditions that so terrified the monks of Christian Europe, must have been prepared to use extreme violence to achieve their ends: *viking* was by definition a violent occupation.

Below: Though the Vikings can no longer be regarded simply as the bloodthirsty plunderers shown in this 19th-century painting by Lorenz Frølich, there can be no doubt that their raids caused great destruction in western Europe, especially to monasteries.

Feeding the Wolves

Were the Viking warriors actually any more violent than their Christian contemporaries? Charlemagne's execution of 4500 Saxon rebels at Verden in 782 shows that the Christians were capable of waging war ruthlessly. As early medieval armies had to live off the land, there can be little doubt either that in wars between Christian states, the peasantry would have suffered greatly from pillaging by enemy armies—and the foraging of "friendly" armies may have been only slightly less destructive. While western Christendom was no stranger to violence, at the time of the outbreak of Viking raiding it was nevertheless more peaceful than it had been at any time since the fall of the western Roman Empire, and, away from disputed borderlands, fortifications of any sort were rare. From being exceptional, the Vikings made violence into an everyday threat for the population of much of western Europe for long periods of time. Even in Ireland, the most anarchic region of western Christendom, the Vikings brought a great increase in the scale of violence. In the period 831–919, Irish sources record only 16 instances of natives plundering and burning, compared to 110 by the Vikings.

The group that arguably suffered the most from Viking raids, the church, was relatively immune from warfare between Christians; even in Ireland, where battles between the monks of rival monasteries were not unknown, churches were rarely plundered. Monasteries were the main centres of literacy in western Christendom, and most of our contemporary accounts of Viking raids were written by monks. According to these sources, Viking raids were often marked by wanton destruction and appalling savagery unparalleled in the knowledge of the writers. It is, of course, possible that some of these accounts may have been exaggerated by the writers' very personal fear and horror of an enemy who made a point of attacking churches, but generally they agree very closely with accounts of Viking raids written in the very different cultural atmospheres of Orthodox Constantinople and the Islamic lands. They also agree very closely with what the Vikings said about themselves. Skaldic poetry of the Viking age glories in bloodshed:

"The destroyer of the Scots fed the wolves: he trod on the eagle's evening meal [of corpses]. The battle-cranes flew over the rows of the slain; the beaks of the birds of prey were not free from blood; the wolf tore wounds and waves of blood surged against the ravens' beaks." (trs. A P. Smyth, *Warlords and Holy Men* London 1984).

Egil Skallagrimsson composed these words in praise of Erik Bloodaxe, but to judge the values of the whole of Scandinavian society on the basis of skaldic verse would be as unwise as it would be to judge late 20th-century western society on the basis of violent movies. However, skaldic verse was composed for an elite warrior audience, and everything else that we know about this class suggests that it accurately reflects its values. It is also from Scandinavian sources that we know of the "blood eagle", the Viking practice of killing captives by hacking through the ribcage on either side of the spine and then tearing the victim's lungs out. This horrific act, of which some historians are oddly reluctant to believe the Vikings capable, may have been performed as a sacrifice to the warriors' god Odin. In fact, it is only common sense to assume that Viking pirates went out of their way to create fear and terror, if only to weaken their victims' will to resist. The ruthless Viking image may not be typical of Viking-age Scandinavian society taken as a whole, but it is certainly representative of an important class within it. Having said this, there is no reason to suppose that the Vikings were uniquely inhuman: they were barbarian warriors, and their behaviour was probably neither better nor worse than that, for example, of the the pagan ancestors of the Franks and Anglo-Saxons who invaded the Roman Empire in the 3rd to 5th centuries.

Fleets and Armies

Western European sources tend to give the strength of the Viking invaders in terms of numbers of ships in their fleets, rather than the number of men in their armies. This raises some obvious problems when used as a basis for calculating the size of the Viking armies. How many men can you get in a ship? Were all Viking ships the same size? How accurately were they counted? To deal with the last question first: when the numbers mentioned in the sources are small, for example the account in the Frankish Royal Annals of a raid by 13 Viking ships in 822, it is reasonable to assume that it is an exact count. With larger fleets there is certainly a much greater likelihood that the figures are an approximation. But at what point can we justifiably begin to suspect exaggeration? There is in fact remarkable consistency between sources from Ireland, Francia and Britain as to the size of Viking fleets. Before 850 fleets of over 100 ships are rarely mentioned, the exceptions being fleets under royal leadership such as Godfred's attack on Frisia with 200 ships in 810. After 850, sources often mention Viking fleets that were 120, 150, 200 or 250 strong, as well as many smaller ones. The tendency has been to accept the smaller figures as reliable and to reject the larger ones as exaggerations, although in most cases the only "evidence" of exaggeration is that the figures are large—a dangerously circular argument. The widespread agreement between independent sources of the same period argues strongly in favour assuming most of the figures, large and small, to be at least approximately accurate. Only in exceptional circumstances can figures from primary sources be rejected outright. For example, the assertion of Abbo, the historian of the siege of Paris in 885–86, that the Viking force numbered 700 ships and 40,000 men is almost certainly a gross exaggeration, because it would have been impossible to keep such a huge army in the field for so long under early medieval conditions.

We do not yet know enough about Viking ships to be able to say how many men they held on average. The 9th-century Gokstad ship was built for a crew of 32 oarsmen, but it was fitted with 32 shields on each side, suggesting a total complement of up to 70 (a double crew would allow rowing in shifts). The slightly later Ladby ship also had 32 oars, but was less broad than the Gokstad ship, and so probably could not carry as many men, while the smaller of the two longships of c. 1000 found at Skuldelev had only 24 oars. If ships were carrying horses, provisions, wives and children, plunder or captives, they would also have carried fewer men than the theoretical maximum. Even so, if we take the smallest of these three ships as being typical, and assume that it carried no supernumeraries, we would still have to conclude that the larger Viking fleets of the later 9th century carried armies of a few thousand warriors rather than the few hundred some historians have argued for. An army of this size would be difficult to keep together for a long time, and the evidence suggests that once a base was established the Viking armies often split up into raiding bands of a few hundred men to plunder the countryside.

Literary and archaeological evidence suggests that the royal fleets that attacked England in the period leading up to the Danish conquest (980–1016) included longships that were rather larger than those used in the 9th century. The larger of the longships from Skuldelev was just such a

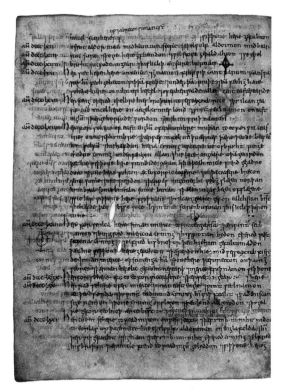

Above: The Anglo-Saxon Chronicle was compiled during the reign of Alfred the Great (871-901) to give an "official" account of events and highlight the leading role of the kings of Wessex in combatting the Vikings. These pages cover the years 862-74, when East Anglia, Northumbria and Mercia were overrun by the Danes.

ship: it had 50 oars and could have carried a complement of 80–100. Even if there were only a few dozen of these "dragon ships" in the fleet of 160 ships Cnut used to invade England in 1016, his army could very easily have numbered 6–7000. By way of comparison, it is estimated that the Norman army at Hastings—which also invaded in a fleet of longships—numbered some 5-6000 men. There were even larger ships available at this time; King Olaf Tryggvason's ship the "Long Serpent" had 68 oars and was capable of carring several hundred men. These dragon ships were probably used mostly for coastal defence, however.

Important further evidence that the Viking armies were not small comes from a document known as the Burghal Hidage, compiled in Wessex around 900. This is a list of the burhs or fortified towns in Wessex, and the number of hides (a measure of land) which were assigned to each for the purposes of garrisoning. The formula used assumed that four men were needed to defend one pole (5 ½ yards) of wall and that one man was to be supplied from each hide assigned to the burh. Wareham, for example, was assigned 1600 hides, meaning that its defences were of such a length as to require 1600 men to man them, that is 400 poles (2200 yards). This corresponds exactly with reality: Wareham's defences still exist, and are 2180 yards in length. Defences would not have been built unless the men were available to man them—walls that were too long to be manned properly would have been worse than useless. As the total number of hides assigned to burhs in Wessex was 27,071, it must be a fair assumption that this number of armed men could be raised by the kingdom of Wessex for garrison duty alone. When it is also taken into account that Alfred the Great kept an army on standby and also had a fleet, the armed strength of Wessex must have been somewhat over 30,000 men. Admittedly they could not all be concentrated in one place at the same time, but it is difficult to believe that a Viking army numbering in the hundreds, rather than the thousands, could have brought Wessex to its knees, let alone conquer all the other Anglo-Saxon kingdoms as well.

On the other hand, the only excavated Viking fortification in Britain, a camp built by the Danish Great Army at Repton in the winter of 873-4, had defences of only 200 yards in length. The enclosed area is therefore small, and could not have accommodated a large force, while the defences could have been manned adequately with a garrison of no more than 150. However, the fort lay on the banks of the River Trent and, as it had a slipway, it may have been built primarily as a protective enclosure for ships rather than as accommodation for the whole army.

A mass burial discovered outside the fort at Repton contained the remains of at least 249 individuals, 80 percent of them males aged 15 to 45. The bones were arranged around a central burial of a high status male, presumably one of the leaders of the Great Army surrounded by his followers. As none had apparently died of injuries, the most likely explanation of the burial is that these were the victims of an epidemic. Pre-modern armies could expect to suffer heavy casualties from disease, and a death rate in winter camp of less than 5 percent would be improbable even in good conditions, and one of more than 35 percent unlikely even in a major epidemic. If the mass burial contains the total Viking dead (the presence of other scattered burials around the site shows that actually it does not), it would point to the Great Army having a minimum strength of 600 and a maximum strength of 4000 men, plus camp followers.

Though a major Viking army of the 9th century may have numbered a few thousand warriors, there certainly were not vast hordes of Vikings streaming out of Scandinavia. Vikings tended to concentrate in particular areas at particular times. When Francia was intensively raided in 879–92, England and Ireland saw little Viking activity, and when the Vikings moved to England in 892, Francia enjoyed a respite. There were rarely more than one or two large Viking forces active at any one time, so total Viking numbers must have been quite limited.

The First Raids

The earliest recorded Viking raids were on England: the first, according to the Anglo-Saxon Chronicle, around 789, was a raid by three ships from

Right: *The martyrdom of St. Edmund, from a 15th-century wall painting in Pickering church, North Yorkshire. The Viking Great Army which invaded England in 865 made short work of the small kingdom of East Anglia. Its king, Edmund, was captured in battle and put to a cruel death. The cult of St. Edmund became popular in the Danelaw after the Viking settlers began to convert to Christianity.*

Norway on Portland in which the reeve Beaduheard and his men were killed. In 792 the great Mercian King Offa arranged coastal defences, presumably against Viking pirates, and in 793 came the shocking raid on the famous monastery founded by St Cuthbert on the Northumbrian island of Lindisfarne, one of the holiest places in the British Isles. The Vikings ransacked the church, killed some of the monks and carried off others into captivity. However, the monastic buildings were not destroyed and many of the monastery's treasures, such as the splendid Lindisfarne Gospels, survived. Presumably the monks had at least a little warning of the attack and were able to hide much of the monastery's wealth before the Vikings struck. It is difficult today to appreciate quite how appalling the attack must have seemed to contemporary Christians. When Alcuin wrote of the attack, "it was not believed that such a voyage was possible," he was not expressing surprise at some hitherto unsuspected seafaring ability on the part of the Vikings—he was well aware of contacts between Northumbria and Scandinavia—but shocked that God and the saints had not intervened to prevent it happening. If somewhere as holy as Lindisfarne was not safe, nowhere was.

The raid on Lindisfarne was typical of the first phase of Viking activity which lasted until around 834. Small fleets of up to about a dozen ships launched uncoordinated raids on the coasts of Britain, Ireland, Frisia and Francia but rarely penetrated more than a few miles inland. Though the speed and mobility enjoyed by the Vikings made such hit-and-run raids hard to prevent, Frankish and Anglo-Saxon resistance was often well organized and effective. All too often, however, the Vikings would have struck and put to sea again by the time a force had been gathered against them. The Irish, who were in a permanent state of anarchic disunity, put up much less effective resistance and suffered severely from Viking raids in this period.

While disunity in western Europe did not cause of the Viking raids—Europe has only rarely been more united—the Vikings were sensitive to political problems and quick to take advantage of them. When civil war broke out in the Frankish empire in 830, with serious consequences for the effectiveness of the coastal defences, Viking raiding entered a new and more serious phase which lasted until 865. Viking fleets became larger (30–35 ships at first, rising to over 100 by the 850s) and bolder, sailing far inland along navigable rivers like the Rhine, Seine, Loire and Shannon to sack major towns. A few raids were also made on Spain and the Mediterranean, though these were not great successes.

In the first phase of Viking activity, raiding had been a seasonal activity with the fleets returning home for the winter. In this second phase the Vikings built camps and began to overwinter in western Europe, allowing an earlier start to raiding the next spring. Permanent settlements were also made in Scotland and Ireland. The Carolingians' dynastic disputes ensured that for most of this period Francia was the focus of Viking activity. The granting of Walcheren as a fief to a troublesome Viking leader in 841 began a period of intermittent Viking rule in Frisia which lasted until the 880s.

Conquest and Settlement

A third phase of Viking activity, characterized by conquest and settlement, began in 865 when a large Viking army invaded East Anglia, shifting the focus of Viking activity to England. After conquering East Anglia, Northumbria and Mercia, the Vikings made extensive settlements in eastern England in the 870s. This period also saw the beginning of the settlement of Iceland, though this was a peaceful affair. The successful resistance of Wessex under Alfred the Great caused those Vikings who did not have the means or the inclination to settle to move their activities back to Francia in the period 879–92. After the Franks made things too hot for them there, the Vikings tried their luck again in England. Alfred the Great had completely reorganized the defences of his kingdom in the previous decade, and the Vikings were harried constantly by the English until their army dispersed in 896, bringing this phase of Viking activity to a close. More effective Irish resistance led to a virtual cessation of Viking activity in Ireland after 874.

The period from 896 to 954 saw a gradual decline in Viking activity. In Francia Rollo and his Vikings were given lands to settle on the lower Seine by Charles the Simple in return for undertaking to keep other Vikings out.

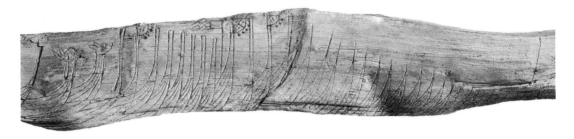

Above: This wood carving shows an impressive fleet of late-Viking ships drawn up on the shore. Contemporary accounts of Viking invasions usually assess the strength of their forces in terms of numbers of ships, making it difficult for modern historians to be sure of the size of Viking armies.

Though there were occasional border troubles, the settlement, which became known as Normandy, effectively ended Viking incursions up the Seine. In 914 the Vikings attempted to create another settlement in continental Europe by conquering Brittany, but in 936 the Bretons drove them out, virtually ending Viking activity on the Continent. Only Frisia, on the main Viking route from Denmark to southeast England, was still raided regularly. Northwest England was settled by Norwegians from around 900, but after this the Vikings were thrown onto the defensive by the kings of Wessex, who had conquered all of the Scandinavian settlements in England by 954. This was not to be the end of Viking activity in England, however; raids began again in the 980s on an increasingly devastating scale. In Ireland, the long hiatus in Viking activity known as the "Forty Years Rest" came to an end in 914. Raiding continued steadily from then on, but the distinction between Viking attacks and internecine conflicts became increasingly blurred as the Scandinavians became absorbed into the indigenous population of Ireland.

The Impact of the Vikings

The Viking raids had a great, sometimes decisive, impact on western Europe. But although the Vikings have been blamed for the break-up of the Carolingian empire, the driving force for this process was internal and dynastic: the Vikings profited from the empire's internal problems but did not cause them. The Vikings usually came a poor second to dynastic concerns in the priorities of the Carolingian rulers, and they were sometimes even welcomed as allies in internecine struggles. Royal measures against the Vikings were often perceived by the Franks to be half-hearted, and by demonstrating the ineffectiveness of royal power, the Vikings may have hastened its decline. The Vikings brought the Franks one certain benefit: their occupation of Brittany in 914–36 broke the power of the native rulers and paved the way for the region's incorporation into Francia. The most important long-term consequence of the Viking involvement in Francia was, however, the establishment of the Duchy of Normandy. Though the Norman expansion of the 11th century cannot be considered an expression of inherited Viking spirit—it was caused by internal political and social developments—its importance to the history of England, France and Italy can hardly be understated.

In England and Scotland, the Vikings broke up the existing power structures with far-reaching consequences for the history of both countries. In Scotland the Viking attacks on the Picts, the Northumbrians and Strathclyde Britons shifted the balance of power in favour of the Scots, allowing them to unify the country. In England the Vikings eliminated the kingdoms of East Anglia, Northumbria and Mercia, leaving Wessex as the sole Anglo-Saxon kingdom. When the Danelaw was conquered by Wessex in the 10th century, the English were, for the first time, united under one crown. Thus both England and Scotland owe their existence as unified states indirectly to the Vikings. The extensive Danish settlements in eastern England have also had a major influence on the development of the English language, which has acquired hundreds of loan words from Old Danish, including ones as basic as sky, egg and sister. Despite this, the Scandinavian settlers in England were absorbed into the native population within 150 years or so. In the Hebrides they preserved their identity a little longer and in Orkney and Shetland, well beyond the end of the Viking age. Aside from the cultural damage caused by attacks on monasteries, the Vikings had surprisingly little effect on Ireland, but they did give the country its first towns and drew it more closely into the European economy.

The effects of the Vikings on the European economy are harder to gauge. Damage to the agricultural economy caused by raids and campaigns is likely to have been short-lived. Towns were built mainly of wood, so although they burned easily, they were also easy to rebuild. Repeated raiding would not be good for their prosperity, but the two main towns which are known to have gone out of existence altogether in the Viking period, Quentovic and Dorestad, probably did so because the rivers which provided access to them silted up, rather than because of Viking attacks. In Ireland and England, the Vikings seem actually to have benefitted trade and promoted urbanization, both directly by founding towns and settlements themselves and indirectly by prompting the Anglo-Saxons to build their fortified burhs.

The most damaging aspect of the Vikings' activities was their attacks on monasteries, which were the main cultural centres of early medieval Europe. Over a large area of northwest Europe, monastic life came to a virtual end. Many monasteries were completely destroyed, others were simply abandoned by their terrified monks. The monastic libraries were destroyed, their books burned or looted for the sake of their decorated covers. Works of art and craftsmanship in precious metals were hacked up and melted down. Perhaps most importantly, the monks—that is the writers, artists and craftsmen themselves—were dispersed, carried off into captivity or killed. The revival of learning fostered by Charlemagne, known as the Carolingian Renaissance, had collapsed before the end of the of the 9th century, while the brilliant monastic culture of early Christian Ireland never recovered from the Viking attacks. Whether this was a long-term setback to European civilization is impossible to say, but the short-term damage to the cultural life of Europe was immense.

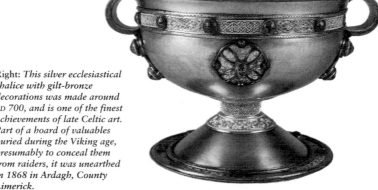

Right: *This silver ecclesiastical chalice with gilt-bronze decorations was made around* AD *700, and is one of the finest achievements of late Celtic art. Part of a hoard of valuables buried during the Viking age, presumably to conceal them from raiders, it was unearthed in 1868 in Ardagh, County Limerick.*

The Raids Begin

The peace and prosperity of 8th-century Europe was shattered by a terrifying new threat from the sea.

"Never before has such an atrocity been seen... The church of St Cuthbert is spattered with the blood of the priests of God, stripped of all its furnishings, exposed to the plundering of pagans—a place more sacred than any in Britain."
Alcuin of York,
AD 793

Viking raids on the British Isles began in the late 780s and began to affect the continent by 799. Initially the Vikings attacked isolated coastal communities and monasteries. Rarely defended, they were easy and profitable targets. According to the Anglo-Saxon Chronicle, the first Viking raid on England took place around 789, when three pirate ships from Norway attacked Portland. In 792 the Mercian King Offa arranged coastal defences for his kingdom; in the following year the famous monastery on Lindisfarne was pillaged. The first raids on Ireland and Scotland were recorded in 795 and the first on Francia in 799.

For the first 30 years or so, the raids were fairly effectively resisted. Both the Anglo-Saxons and the Franks recognized that the greatest danger was that the Vikings would sail upriver and penetrate inland. The Anglo-Saxons blocked the rivers with bridges, while the Frankish emperor Charlemagne stationed coastguards and fleets on them. However, there was little that could be done to protect exposed coastal areas like Frisia. In 810, the Danish King Godfred, feeling threatened by Frankish expansion on his border, ravaged the empire's vulnerable Frisian coast: by the time the Franksih fleet and army had gathered, the raiders were long gone. Like an earlier attack on the Franks' Slav allies, the Abodrites, this was as much a show of strength as a plundering expedition. After his death in 815, Charlemagne's successor Louis the Pious at first continued to maintain effective coast defences. However, in the 830s, the empire was riven by internal conflicts, and its defences weakened. By 840 the Vikings had penetrated the Rhine four times to sack Dorestad, the empire's richest port.

Right: *the Viking raid on the monastery at Lindisfarne is vividly depicted on this 9th-century tombstone from the priory there. The attack sent shock waves through Europe: why had God allowed such a holy place to be defiled by pagans? Were the Vikings a punishment for some terrible sin?*

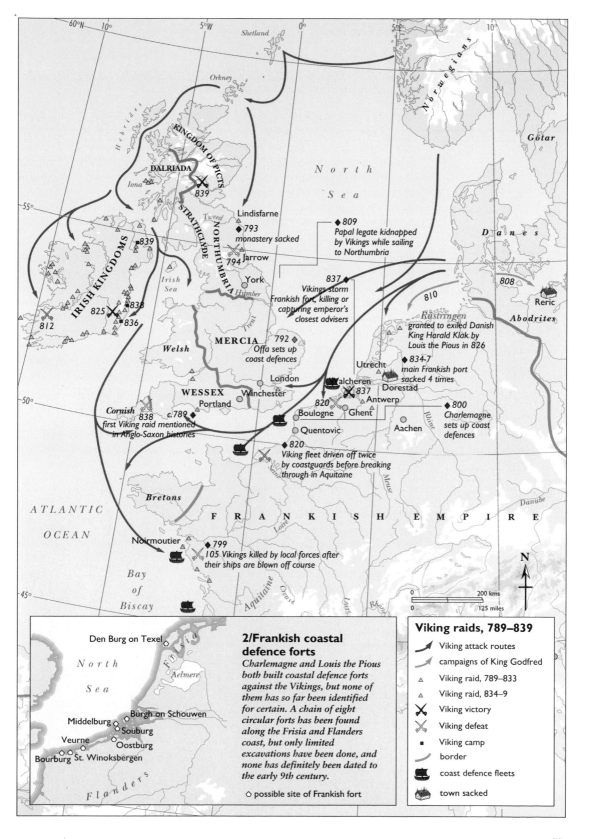

Shetland

Orkney

Norwegians

Götar

KINGDOM OF PICTS

DALRIADA

Iona

839

Hebrides

Tweed

STRATHCLYDE

NORTHUMBRIA

Lindisfarne

◆ 793
monastery sacked

794 Jarrow

York

Humber

N o r t h

S e a

Danes

◆ 809
Papal legate kidnapped
by Vikings while sailing
to Northumbria

808

Reric

Abodrites

839

IRISH KINGDOMS

Irish
Sea

825 ■ 838
× 836

812

Trent

MERCIA

792 ◆
Offa sets up
coast defences

Welsh

London

WESSEX

Portland

Winchester

Cornish
838 c.789 ◆
first Viking raid mentioned
in Anglo-Saxon histories

◆ 837
Vikings storm
Frankish fort, killing or
capturing emperor's
closest advisers

810

Rüstringen
granted to exiled Danish
King Harald Klak by
Louis the Pious in 826

Utrecht

◆ 834-7
main Frankish port
sacked 4 times

Walcheren ◆ 837
× 820 Dorestad
Boulogne Ghent Antwerp
Quentovic Aachen

Rhine

◆ 800
Charlemagne
sets up coast
defences

◆ 820
Viking fleet driven off twice
by coastguards before breaking
through in Aquitaine

Meuse

Danube

Bretons

A T L A N T I C

O C E A N

F R A N K I S H   E M P I R E

Loire

Aquitaine

Creuse

Loire

Rhine

N

◆ 799
105 Vikings killed by local forces after
their ships are blown off course

Noirmoutier

Bay
of
Biscay

0   200 kms
0   125 miles

Viking raids, 789–839

⟿ Viking attack routes

⟿ campaigns of King Godfred

△ Viking raid, 789–833

△ Viking raid, 834–9

✕ Viking victory

⚔ Viking defeat

■ Viking camp

border

coast defence fleets

town sacked

The Raids Intensify

Civil war among the Franks allowed Viking raiders to sail upriver and strike deep into the heart of Francia.

"A very hard winter. In March, 120 ships of the Northmen sailed up the Seine to Paris, laying waste to everything ... Charles ... realized his men could not possibly win. So he made a deal... by handing over 7000 lb of silver ... he persuaded them to go away."
The Annals of St Bertin, AD 845

As soon as the Frankish emperor Louis the Pious died in 840, his three sons—Lothar, Charles the Bald and Louis the German—fell out over their inheritance. The Vikings were quick to exploit political weakness, and raids became more frequent. The civil wars damaged royal authority, and the coastal defences created by Charlemagne collapsed. The great rivers of the empire lay open to Viking fleets which could penetrate far inland, sacking major towns, ports and inland monasteries. From being a seasonal threat, the Vikings now became a permanent presence, seizing river islands such as Oissel in the Seine to use as bases for prolonged campaigns of raiding.

Charles the Bald's kingdom, with its long coastline and many navigable rivers, was hit the worst. The Vikings benefited from his internal problems: in 843 a rebel count allied with them to seize Nantes, and in 858 his brother Louis the German invaded, forcing Charles to abandon a siege of the Viking base at Oissel. Charles was forced to pay 'Danegeld' to buy the Vikings off. In the long term this only encouraged more raids, but it bought him time to deal with his internal enemies. Sometimes the Vikings could be a help—their attack on Bordeaux in 848 discredited the rebel prince who controlled the city, enabling Charles to restore his authority there.

Lothar's kingdom included Frisia and the Rhine estuary, both frequent targets of Viking raids. Lothar solved his Viking problem by granting lands in these areas to Viking chiefs on condition that they kept other Vikings out. These Vikings were unreliable allies, but there were no raids further down the Rhine than Dorestad before 863. The eastern kingdom of Louis the German, with only a short coastline, had little trouble from the Vikings. England also remained relatively untroubled by raids. The Anglo-Saxons inflicted some severe defeats on the Vikings in this period, making England an unattractive target in comparison to Francia.

Right: *Charles the Bald, King of the West Franks (843–77), shown seated on his throne from the frontispiece of a contemporary Bible.*

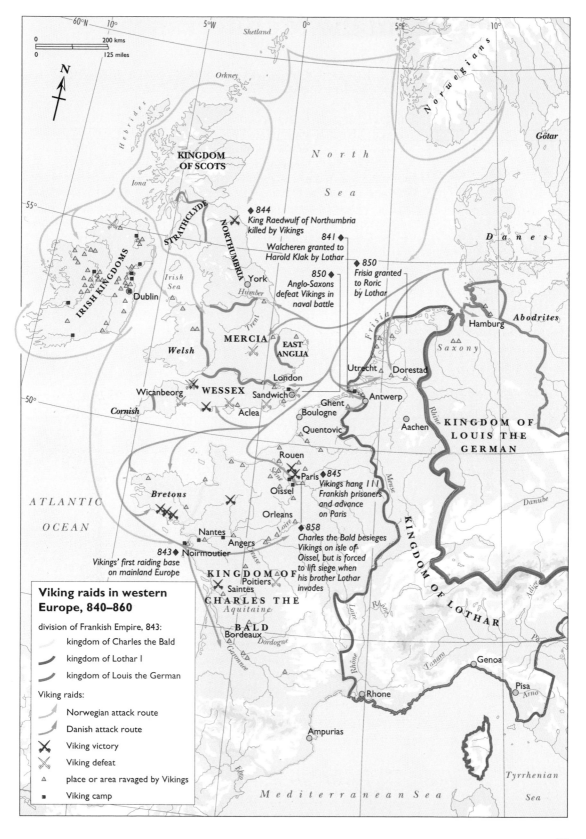

0   200 kms
0   125 miles

N

Shetland

Orkney

Hebrides

**KINGDOM
OF SCOTS**

Iona

*Irish
Sea*

STRATHCLYDE

NORTHUMBRIA

◆ 844
King Raedwulf of Northumbria
killed by Vikings

York
Humber

IRISH KINGDOMS

Dublin

N o r t h

S e a

Norwegians

Götar

D a n e s

◆ 841
Walcheren granted to
Harold Klak by Lothar

850 ◆
Anglo-Saxons
defeat Vikings in
naval battle

◆ 850
Frisia granted
to Roric
by Lothar

Hamburg

Abodrites

Saxony

Frisia

Trent

MERCIA

**EAST
ANGLIA**

Welsh

London

WESSEX

Wicanbeorg

Cornish

Sandwich
Aclea

Utrecht

Ghent
Boulogne

Quentovic

Antwerp

Dorestad

Aachen

**KINGDOM OF
LOUIS THE
GERMAN**

Rhine

A T L A N T I C

O C E A N

Bretons

Rouen

Paris ◆ 845
Vikings hang
Frankish prisoners
and advance
on Paris

Oissel

Orleans

Seine

Loire

◆ 858
Charles the Bald besieges
Vikings on isle of
Oissel, but is forced
to lift siege when
his brother Lothar
invades

Nantes

Angers

843 ◆ Noirmoutier
*Vikings' first raiding base
on mainland Europe*

KINGDOM OF

Poitiers
Saintes

CHARLES THE

Aquitaine

BALD

Bordeaux

Dordogne

Garonne

Meuse

Danube

**KINGDOM
OF
LOTHAR**

Rhône

Loire

Tanaro

Adige

Po

Genoa

Pisa
Arno

Rhône

Ampurias

*Tyrrhenian
Sea*

M e d i t e r r a n e a n   S e a

**Viking raids in western
Europe, 840–860**

division of Frankish Empire, 843:

    kingdom of Charles the Bald

    kingdom of Lothar I

    kingdom of Louis the German

Viking raids:

    Norwegian attack route

    Danish attack route

✕   Viking victory

✕   Viking defeat

△   place or area ravaged by Vikings

■   Viking camp

The Vikings in the Mediterranean

Viking fleets raided Christian and Muslim Spain, and struck deep into the Mediterranean.

Only a year after they had established a base at the mouth of the Loire, the Vikings turned their attention to Spain. A fleet of around 100 ships left the Loire and pillaged on the Garonne before descending on the Spanish Christian Kingdom of Galicia and Asturias. Local resistance was effective, and the Vikings moved on round Cape Finisterre, to try their luck against the Umayyad Emirate of Cordoba. The Vikings took Lisbon virtually unopposed, then, after sacking Cadiz and Medina Sidonia, they sailed up the

"They came afterwards across ... the place where the Mediterranean goes into the outer ocean and reached Africa. They gave battle to the Moors, and a great slaughter was made... After that the Norsemen brought a great host of Moors in captivity with them to Ireland... Long were these blue men in Ireland."
Duald Mac-Fuirbis on Hastein and Bjorn's raids, AD 859–62

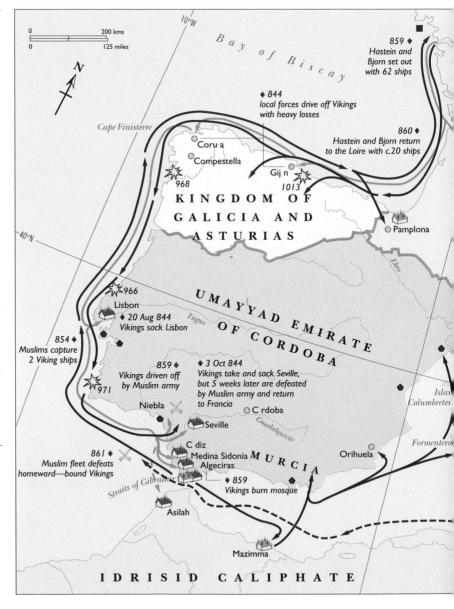

*859 ♦
Hastein and Bjorn set out with 62 ships*

*♦ 844
local forces drive off Vikings with heavy losses*

*860 ♦
Hastein and Bjorn return to the Loire with c.20 ships*

Cape Finisterre

Coruña
Compostella

Gijón

968   1013

KINGDOM OF GALICIA AND ASTURIAS

Pamplona

Ebro

966

Lisbon
*♦ 20 Aug 844
Vikings sack Lisbon*

Tagus

UMAYYAD EMIRATE OF CORDOBA

*854 ♦
Muslims capture 2 Viking ships*

*859 ♦
Vikings driven off by Muslim army*

*♦ 3 Oct 844
Vikings take and sack Seville, but 5 weeks later are defeated by Muslim army and return to Francia*

Córdoba

Guadalquivir

971

Niebla

Seville

Islas Columbretes

Formentera

Cádiz
Medina Sidonia
Algeciras

MURCIA

Orihuela

*861 ♦
Muslim fleet defeats homeward—bound Vikings*

Straits of Gibraltar

*859
Vikings burn mosque*

Asilah

Mazimma

IDRISID CALIPHATE

The capital of Muslim Spain was at Cordoba, where the Great Mosque (above) was begun in 785. The Vikings were no match for this powerful, well-organized and highly motivated state.

River Guadalquivir and captured Seville. From there they raided the sur-rounding countryside until, five weeks later, the Vikings were heavily defeat-ed by a Muslim army: the Muslims claimed to have destroyed 30 ships, killed 1000 men and taken 400 prisoners, most of whom were later executed. The survivors surrendered their captives and booty and were glad to escape back to the Loire with their lives.

Thirteen years later the Vikings returned to Spain with 62 ships under Hastein and Bjorn Ironsides, two of the most famous Viking leaders. At first they had as little luck as their predecessors, being soundly beaten by both the Asturians and Muslims as they cruised south along Spain's Atlantic coast. However, at the Straits of Gibraltar the Vikings' luck changed. Algeciras was sacked, then the coasts of Morocco, Murcia, the Balearic Islands and Rousillon were ravaged. They spent the winter of 859–60 on the island of Camargue, at the mouth of the Rhone, before ravaging upstream as far as Valence the following spring. But resistance was fierce, so the Vikings moved on to Italy, sacking Luna (believing it to be Rome) and sail-ing up the River Arno to sack Pisa and Fiesole. After this Hastein and Bjorn are said to have to sailed into the eastern Mediterranean, but their move-ments are uncertain until 861, when they were again defeated by a Muslim fleet off Spain. Finally, Pamplona was sacked before the 20 surviving ships made it back to the Loire in 862. It had been a mighty feat but very costly. The Vikings preferred easier targets: in the future Spain was only rarely raid-ed, and the Vikings never returned to the Mediterranean.

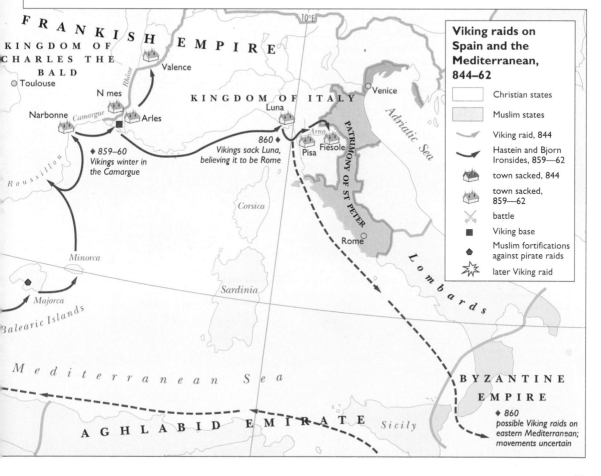

Viking raids on Spain and the Mediterranean, 844–62

	Christian states
	Muslim states
	Viking raid, 844
	Hastein and Bjorn Ironsides, 859—62
	town sacked, 844
	town sacked, 859—62
	battle
	Viking base
	Muslim fortifications against pirate raids
	later Viking raid

FRANKISH EMPIRE

KINGDOM OF CHARLES THE BALD

Toulouse

Valence

Rhône

N mes

Narbonne *Camargue*

Arles

859–60
Vikings winter in the Camargue

Roussillon

KINGDOM OF ITALY

Luna

Arno

860
Vikings sack Luna, believing it to be Rome

Pisa Fiesole

Venice

Adriatic Sea

PATRIMONY OF ST PETER

Corsica

Rome

Lombards

Minorca

Majorca

Sardinia

Balearic Islands

Mediterranean Sea

BYZANTINE EMPIRE

860
possible Viking raids on eastern Mediterranean; movements uncertain

AGHLABID EMIRATE *Sicily*

The Franks Fight Back

By 859 Charles the Bald had survived the worst crises of his reign and could turn his attention to the Vikings, who now posed a serious threat to the economy of the Frankish heartlands.

"Charles caused all the leading men of his realm to assemble about 1 June, with many workmen and carts, at the place called Pitres, where the Andelle... and the Eure... flow into the Seine, he closed it off to ships sailing up or down the river. This was done because of the Northmen."
The Annals of St Bertin, AD 862

New fortifications were built, Roman town walls were restored, and fortified bridges constructed across the rivers Seine and Loire. But the bridges were positioned well inland, and while they protected Paris and the Frankish heartlands, they effectively abandoned the lower reaches of both rivers to the Vikings.

Charles's army was still unreliable—it ran away from the Vikings in 866—but his siege of the Vikings in Angers in 873 was a notable victory. He also tried to play one Viking army off against another. In 860 he hired the services of Weland, a Viking chief based on the Somme, to attack the Seine Vikings at their base on Oissel. The Seine Vikings offered Weland a huge bribe to let them escape, and the next year they were back again, raiding on the Marne. The Vikings only left the Seine in 866 after Charles had resorted to the old expedient of paying Danegeld.

Increasingly the most effective defence came not from the king but from local leaders. The Loire Vikings suffered a number of sharp defeats in the 860s at the hands of local counts, who could react more quickly than centralized royal forces. By the end of the 9th century, they had become the basis of Frankish defence. There were limits to the devolution of defence, however, and peasant bands which had formed in 859 to fight the Vikings were suppressed by the counts. This stiffening of Frankish resistance certainly contributed to the decline of Viking activity in the late 860s, but it was the success of the Danish Great Army which invaded England in 865 that more than anything turned Viking attentions away from Francia.

Bri

2/The fortified bridge at Pont de l'Arche

The key to Charles the Bald's defences for the Seine was the fortified bridge at Pont de l'Arche near Pitres. The bridge was protected by garrisons stationed in large forts of wood and stone on both banks of the river. Construction was begun in 862, but work was slow and the unfinished bridge was under Viking control in 865. Work on the bridge and its forts was finally completed around 870. A Viking fleet which entered the Seine in 876 did not get past the bridge, and the Vikings stayed away for the next ten years. The bridge and fort were eventually destroyed in a Viking attack in 885.

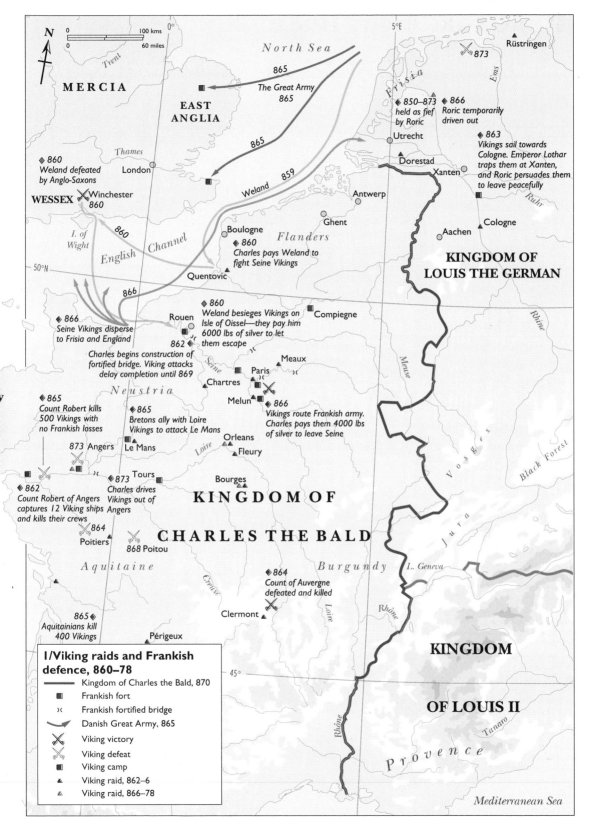

N

0 ——— 100 kms
0 ——— 60 miles

North Sea

865
The Great Army
865

865

865

859

Trent

MERCIA

EAST ANGLIA

Thames

London

◆ 860
Weland defeated
by Anglo-Saxons

WESSEX ✗ Winchester
860

Weland

I. of Wight

English Channel

860

866

Quentovic ▲

860

◆ 866
Seine Vikings disperse
to Frisia and England

Rouen ◌

862 ◆

Seine

Charles begins construction of
fortified bridge. Viking attacks
delay completion until 869

Neustria

◆ 865
Count Robert kills
500 Vikings with
no Frankish losses

◆ 865
Bretons ally with Loire
Vikings to attack Le Mans

873 Angers
▲ ■✗ Le Mans

◆ 862
Count Robert of Angers
captures 12 Viking ships
and kills their crews

■ ✗

✗ 864
Poitiers

◆ 873
Tours
Charles drives
Vikings out of
Angers

868 Poitou

Aquitaine

865 ◆
Aquitainians kill
400 Vikings

Périgueux

◆ 860
Charles pays Weland to
fight Seine Vikings

Boulogne
◌

Flanders

Ghent ◌

Antwerp ◌

Utrecht ◌

Frisia

✗ 873

Rüstringen ■

Ems

◆ 850–873
held as fief
by Roric

◆ 866
Roric temporarily
driven out

◆ 863
Vikings sail towards
Cologne. Emperor Lothar
traps them at Xanten,
and Roric persuades them
to leave peacefully

Dorestad ◌
Xanten ◆

■

Aachen ▲

Cologne ▲

Ruhr

**KINGDOM OF
LOUIS THE GERMAN**

Rhine

5°E

◆ 860
Weland besieges Vikings on
Isle of Oissel—they pay him
6000 lbs of silver to let
them escape

Compiegne ■

Meaux ▲

Paris ■
Chartres ▲
Melun ■✗

◆ 866
Vikings route Frankish army.
Charles pays them 4000 lbs
of silver to leave Seine

Meuse

50°N

Orleans ▲
▲ Fleury

Bourges ▲▲

KINGDOM OF

CHARLES THE BALD

◆ 864
Count of Auvergne
defeated and killed

Clermont ▲

Burgundy

L. Geneva ◌

Loire

Creuse

Vosges

Jura

Black Forest

Rhône

45°

KINGDOM

OF LOUIS II

Tanaro

Provence

Mediterranean Sea

1/Viking raids and Frankish defence, 860–78

——— Kingdom of Charles the Bald, 870
■ Frankish fort
)(Frankish fortified bridge
⌒ Danish Great Army, 865
✗ Viking victory
✗ Viking defeat
■ Viking camp
▲ Viking raid, 862–6
▲ Viking raid, 866–78

The Great Army in England

A great Danish army arrives in England, and one by one the Saxon kingdoms fell to the invaders.

"In this year the host went across Mercia into East Anglia ... St Edmund the king fought against them, and the Danes won ... they slew the king and overran the entire kingdom, and destroyed all the monasteries to which they came."
The Anglo-Saxon Chronicle, AD 869

For most of the 9th century, England seems to have escaped the worst of the Viking raids that plagued Ireland and Francia. But it was vulnerable—divided into small, uncooperative kingdoms which could be picked off one at a time, and crisscrossed by Roman roads along which an invader could move quickly. When the Danes did arrive in force, their intention was not merely plunder, but conquest. In 865 a "great heathen army" under the command of Ivar and Halfdan arrived in East Anglia. The kingdom bought peace with a supply of horses, and in 866 the Danes rode north. The Northumbrians were preoccupied with a civil war, and the Danes entered York unopposed. The following spring, the two rival kings united to try to recapture York, but the attack failed and they were both killed. The kingdom of Northumbria died with them: by 876 York had become capital of a new Viking kingdom.

In 867 the Danes forayed into Mercia. A joint Mercian-West Saxon force besieged them at Nottingham—the only time that one Anglo-Saxon kingdom helped another against the Danes—and they withdrew to York. The Danes returned to East Anglia in 869, where they defeated and killed King Edmund, bringing a second Anglo-Saxon kingdom under their control. The next year they invaded Wessex. King Æthelræd and his brother Alfred resisted fiercely; the Danes withdrew to London, then back to York. They invaded Mercia again in 873, and the kingdom collapsed after the Danes took the royal centre of Repton. Here the army split: Halfdan returned to consolidate his hold on York, while the other half under Guthrum, Oscetel and Anund went to Cambridge before invading Wessex in 875. Alfred, now king, was forced to take refuge in the Somerset marshes. But the Danes had been weakened by the division of the army, and by the fact that many of their fighters had decided to settle on the lands they had won in Northumbria and Mercia. When Alfred managed to raise another army and won a great victory at Eddington, the Danes agreed to leave Wessex.

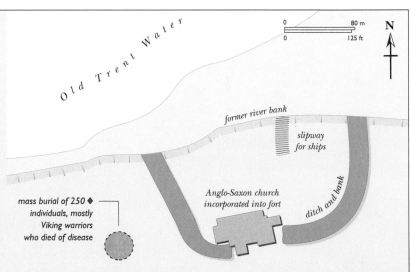

2/The Viking fort at Repton
Viking armies chose defensible positions for their winter camps with at least one side defended by water or marshland. The small camp at Repton was built for the Great Army in the winter of 873–4. The river Trent protected one side of the camp, the other was defended by a D-shaped rampart and ditch which incorporated an Anglo-Saxon monastic church. A slipway in the fort suggests that ships were beached inside the enclosure for protection.

Old Trent Water

former river bank

slipway for ships

mass burial of 250 ♦ individuals, mostly Viking warriors who died of disease

Anglo-Saxon church incorporated into fort

ditch and bank

0   80 m
0   125 ft

N

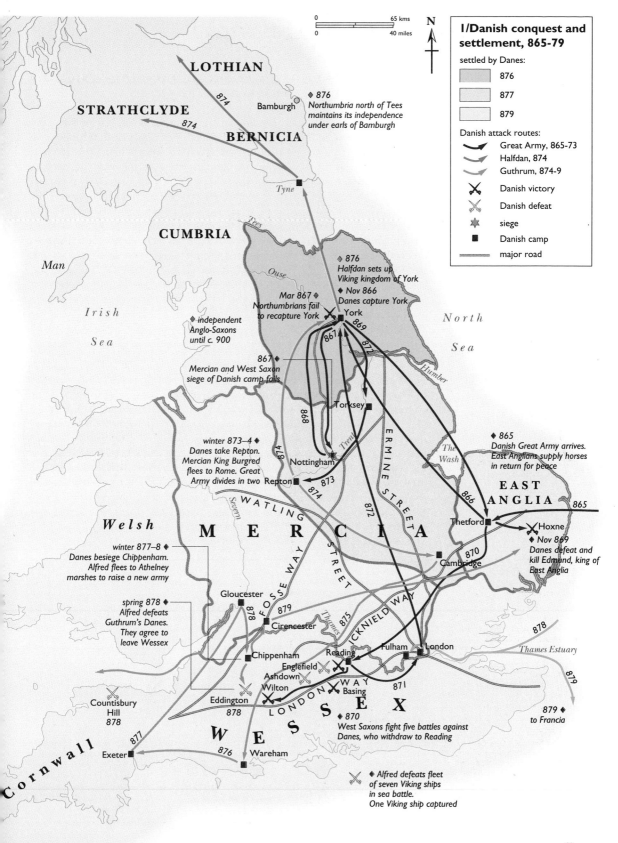

0   65 kms
0   40 miles

N

1/Danish conquest and settlement, 865-79

settled by Danes:
- 876
- 877
- 879

Danish attack routes:
- Great Army, 865-73
- Halfdan, 874
- Guthrum, 874-9
- ✕ Danish victory
- ✕ Danish defeat
- ✦ siege
- ■ Danish camp
- major road

LOTHIAN

STRATHCLYDE

874

874

Bamburgh ◇ 876

BERNICIA

◇ 876
Northumbria north of Tees
maintains its independence
under earls of Bamburgh

Tyne

CUMBRIA

Tees

Man

Ouse

◇ 876
Halfdan sets up
Viking kingdom of York

Irish
Sea

Mar 867 ◇
Northumbrians fail
to recapture York

◇ Nov 866
Danes capture York

York

North
Sea

867
861
869
874

◆ independent
Anglo-Saxons
until c. 900

867 ◆
Mercian and West Saxon
siege of Danish camp fails

868

Torksey

◆ 865
Danish Great Army arrives.
East Anglians supply horses
in return for peace

Humber

866

874

winter 873–4 ◆
Danes take Repton.
Mercian King Burgred
flees to Rome. Great
Army divides in two

Nottingham

Trent

872

ERMINE STREET

The
Wash

Repton

873

874

EAST
ANGLIA

865

Welsh

WATLING

MERCIA

Thetford

870

✕ Hoxne

◆ Nov 869
Danes defeat and
kill Edmund, king of
East Anglia

winter 877–8 ◆
Danes besiege Chippenham.
Alfred flees to Athelney
marshes to raise a new army

FOSSE WAY

STREET

Cambridge

spring 878 ◆
Alfred defeats
Guthrum's Danes.
They agree to
leave Wessex

Gloucester

878

879

Cirencester

Thames

875

ICKNIELD WAY

Fulham

London

878

Chippenham

Reading

871

Thames Estuary

Englefield

Ashdown

Wilton

LONDON WAY

Basing

879

879 ◆
to Francia

Countisbury
Hill
878

Eddington

878

W E S S E X

◆ 870
West Saxons fight five battles against
Danes, who withdraw to Reading

877

876

Cornwall

Exeter

Wareham

✕ ◆ Alfred defeats fleet
of seven Viking ships
in sea battle.
One Viking ship captured

The Great Raids on Francia

Alfred the Great's successful defence of Wessex is bad news for Francia as the Vikings seek easier pickings there.

"The Northmen continue to kill and take Christian people captive; without ceasing they destroy churches and dwellings and burn towns. Along all the roads one sees bodies of the clergy and laity, of nobles and others, of women, children and infants."
Annals of St Vaast, 884

The Viking fleet which had arrived on the Thames in 878 crossed the sea the following year and landed near Calais. The Vikings acquired horses and plundered northern Flanders on their way to Ghent, where they were joined by their ships in a winter camp. This set a pattern for the next 12 years: every year the Vikings moved on to a new camp, usually located at a monastery on a navigable river, and used it as a base from which to raid the surrounding countryside. For five years Flanders, the Rhineland and Picardy were methodically ravaged. When these were exhausted the Vikings moved south and sailed up the Seine to Paris in 885. Two fortified bridges blocked their way. The Viking leader Sigfrid demanded safe passage, but the Parisians refused. The Vikings attempted to destroy the bridges but, encouraged by their bishop Joscelin and their count Odo, the defenders held out for almost a year before the city was relieved by Emperor Charles the Fat. Instead of attacking the Vikings, however, Charles simply gave them the permission they wanted to sail past Paris. They spent the next two years raiding along the Marne and upper Seine. Charles's pusillanimous act led to his deposition and the final breakup of the Carolingian empire in 888.

The West Franks now chose as king a man who had proven his fighting spirit, Count Odo, the hero of Paris. With an effective display of force and the encouragement of a payment of Danegeld, Odo rid the Seine of Vikings in 889. The Vikings now launched an unsuccessful invasion of Brittany before moving back to try their luck in the East Frankish kingdom. The East Franks' chosen successor to Charles the Fat, Arnulf, was another man like Odo, and the Vikings faced resistance wherever they went. The Franks had built fortresses and town walls across the whole area between the Seine and the Rhine. The final straw was a severe famine which affected Francia in 891–2; it was probably this, more than military pressure, that forced the main Viking army to leave for England in 892. Francia had not seen the last of the Vikings, but the worst of the raids were now past.

ET SY RIAM SOBAL· ET CONVERTIT
IOAB· ET PERCVSSIT EDOM INVAL
LESALINARVM·XII MILIA·

The heavily armed Frankish cavalry was potentially the most powerful force in Europe. However, low morale – the result of political instability and poor leadership – often led to the Franks being routed by the Vikings.

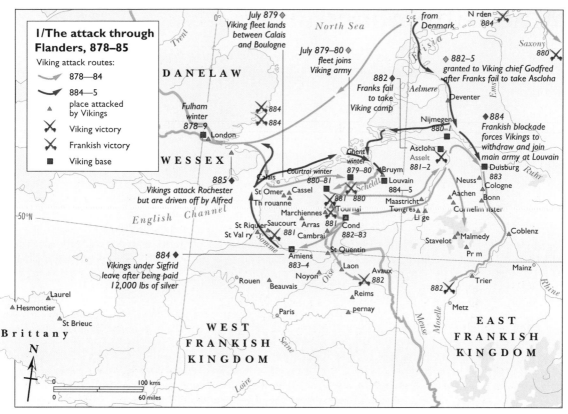

1/The attack through Flanders, 878–85

Viking attack routes:
- 878—84
- 884—5
- ▲ place attacked by Vikings
- ✕ Viking victory
- ✕ Frankish victory
- ■ Viking base

July 879 ◆ Viking fleet lands between Calais and Boulogne

July 879–80 ◆ fleet joins Viking army

from Denmark

N rden 884

Saxony 880

◆ 882–5 granted to Viking chief Godfred after Franks fail to take Ascloha

882 ◆ Franks fail to take Viking camp

◆ 884 Frankish blockade forces Vikings to withdraw and join main army at Louvain

884 ◆ Frankish blockade forces Vikings to withdraw and join main army at Louvain

North Sea

Fulham winter 878–9

DANELAW

London

WESSEX

885 ◆ Vikings attack Rochester but are driven off by Alfred

Calais

Ghent winter 879–80

Courtrai winter 880–81

St Omer
Th rouanne
Cassel

Marchiennes

St Riquier
St Val ry
Saucourt
Arras
Cambrai

Amiens 883–4

884 ◆ Vikings under Sigfrid leave after being paid 12,000 lbs of silver

Laurel
Hesmontier
St Brieuc

Brittany

N

English Channel

50°N

Rouen
Beauvais

Noyon
Laon

Reims

pernay

WEST FRANKISH KINGDOM

Paris

Seine

Loire

100 kms
60 miles

Aelmere

Deventer

Nijmegen 880–1

Ascloha
Asselt 881–2

Bruym

Louvain 884–5

Tournai 881 880

Cond 882–83

Maastricht
Tongres
Li ge

Duisburg 883
Neuss
Cologne
Aachen
Bonn
Cornelim nster

Stavelot

Malmedy
Pr m

Coblenz

Mainz

St Quentin

Avaux 882

882

Trier

Metz

EAST FRANKISH KINGDOM

Rhine

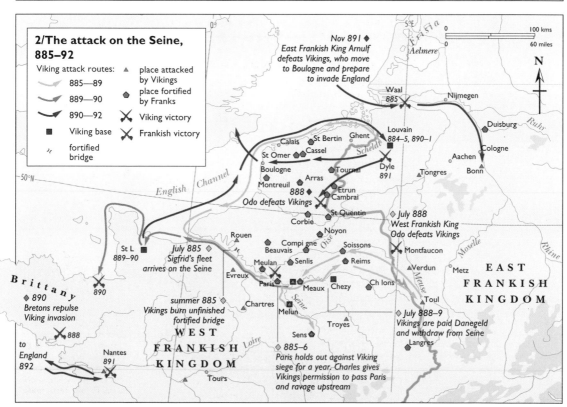

2/The attack on the Seine, 885–92

Viking attack routes:
- 885—89
- 889—90
- 890—92
- ■ Viking base
- ⌇ fortified bridge
- ▲ place attacked by Vikings
- ⬠ place fortified by Franks
- ✕ Viking victory
- ✕ Frankish victory

Nov 891 ◆ East Frankish King Arnulf defeats Vikings, who move to Boulogne and prepare to invade England

Waal 885

Nijmegen

Duisburg

Cologne

Louvain 884–5, 890–1

Aachen

Bonn

Calais
St Bertin
Ghent
Cassel

St Omer

Boulogne
Montreuil
Arras

Tournai

Etrun
Cambrai
888 ◆ Odo defeats Vikings

Dyle 891

Tongres

Corbie

St Quentin

Noyon

◆ July 888 West Frankish King Odo defeats Vikings

St L 889–90

July 885 ◆ Sigfrid's fleet arrives on the Seine

Rouen

Compi gne

Beauvais

Meulan
Evreux
Senlis

Paris

Soissons

Reims

Montfaucon

Verdun

Metz

Toul

EAST FRANKISH KINGDOM

summer 885 ◆ Vikings burn unfinished fortified bridge

Chartres

Meaux

Chezy

Ch lons

Melun

Brittany

◆ 890 Bretons repulse Viking invasion

888

to England 892

Nantes 891

Tours

WEST FRANKISH KINGDOM

Troyes

Sens

◆ July 888–9 Vikings are paid Danegeld and withdraw from Seine

885–6 ◆ Paris holds out against Viking siege for a year, Charles gives Vikings permission to pass Paris and ravage upstream

Langres

Loire

Seine

Meuse

Moselle

Rhine

English Channel

50°N

Frisia
Aelmere

100 kms
60 miles

N

Wessex Defended

The departure of the Great Army gave Wessex a breathing space, and when the Vikings returned they found conditions utterly changed.

"Then the English army arrived and put the Viking army to flight and stormed the fortification [of Benfleet] and seized everything that was inside it in the way of goods, women and children as well ... Hastein's wife and his two sons were brought to the king; and he gave them back again, because one was his godson and the other the godson of Ealdorman Æthelræd."
The Anglo-Saxon Chronicle, AD 893

After the Danes left for the continent in 879, Alfred reorganized the *fyrd*, or peasant militia, so that it could stay in the field for longer. The royal army also became much more mobile, and was able to react quickly to Viking attacks. A fleet was built to challenge the Vikings on the high seas. Most important was the construction of a network of *burhs*—fortified settlements—across the whole of Wessex. The overall effect of these measures was to deny the Viking armies the freedom of movement which they had enjoyed in the 860s and 870s, and make them much more vulnerable to counter-attack. The acceptance by the Mercians of Alfred's leadership in 886 also ensured a greater degree of cooperation between the Anglo-Saxons than had existed before.

The Vikings continued to hold the initiative, however, and had the great advantage of being able to retreat into friendly Danish-held territory if they suffered a reverse. The Danes of Northumbria and the Danelaw also supplied reinforcements and launched diversionary raids on the coasts of Wessex. Despite this, the two Viking armies which arrived in Kent in 892 were not destined to prosper. The only major raid into Wessex was defeated in spring 893 and when, shortly after, the two Viking armies joined up at Benfleet in Essex they had no sooner gone on a raid than the English captured their camp, together with their families and loot. Their ships were either destroyed or taken to London and Rochester by the English. A raid deep into Mercia later in the year also ended in defeat and the Vikings were lucky to escape into the Danelaw. Late in 893 the Vikings took Chester, but the English destroyed the local food supplies and hunger forced them into Wales. To avoid English forces, they returned to their East Anglian base through Northumbria in 894.

The Viking army now moved to the River Lea, threatening London, but Alfred blockaded the river and forced it to abandon its ships and flee overland into Mercia in 895. After spending another winter under siege at Bridgnorth, the frustrated Viking army broke up: some settled in Northumbria and East Anglia, others returned to Francia. After their departure the Anglo-Saxon chronicler heaved a sigh of relief: "the Viking army had not—by God's grace!—afflicted the English people to a very great extent" he concluded. Though the English had not won any great victories, they had prevented the Vikings from plundering at will, and at no time had Alfred's defences looked likely to break down.

Right: the Alfred Jewel was made as a handle to a pointer, intended to be used as an aid to reading. Alfred actively promoted education and monasticism in the belief that moral and spiritual defences were as necessary to his kingdom as physical defences, such as the burhs.

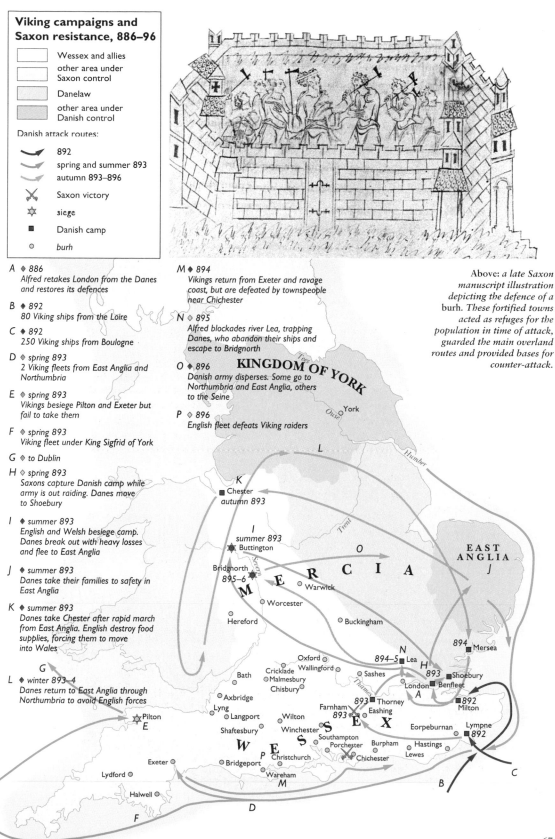

Viking campaigns and Saxon resistance, 886–96

	Wessex and allies
	other area under Saxon control
	Danelaw
	other area under Danish control

Danish attack routes:

- 892
- spring and summer 893
- autumn 893–896
- ✗ Saxon victory
- ✡ siege
- ■ Danish camp
- ○ burh

A ◆ 886
Alfred retakes London from the Danes and restores its defences

B ◆ 892
80 Viking ships from the Loire

C ◆ 892
250 Viking ships from Boulogne

D ◇ spring 893
2 Viking fleets from East Anglia and Northumbria

E ◇ spring 893
Vikings besiege Pilton and Exeter but fail to take them

F ◇ spring 893
Viking fleet under King Sigfrid of York

G ◇ to Dublin

H ◇ spring 893
Saxons capture Danish camp while army is out raiding. Danes move to Shoebury

I ◆ summer 893
English and Welsh besiege camp. Danes break out with heavy losses and flee to East Anglia

J ◆ summer 893
Danes take their families to safety in East Anglia

K ◆ summer 893
Danes take Chester after rapid march from East Anglia. English destroy food supplies, forcing them to move into Wales

L ◆ winter 893–4
Danes return to East Anglia through Northumbria to avoid English forces

M ◆ 894
Vikings return from Exeter and ravage coast, but are defeated by townspeople near Chichester

N ◇ 895
Alfred blockades river Lea, trapping Danes, who abandon their ships and escape to Bridgnorth

O ◆ 896
Danish army disperses. Some go to Northumbria and East Anglia, others to the Seine

P ◇ 896
English fleet defeats Viking raiders

Above: *a late Saxon manuscript illustration depicting the defence of a burh. These fortified towns acted as refuges for the population in time of attack, guarded the main overland routes and provided bases for counter-attack.*

KINGDOM OF YORK

York

L

K ■ Chester autumn 893

I summer 893 ✡ Buttington

Bridgnorth 895–6

MERCIA

Warwick

Worcester

Hereford

Buckingham

EAST ANGLIA **J**

O

894 ■ Mersea

Oxford

Cricklade
Malmesbury
Chisbury

Wallingford

Sashes

894–5 ■ Lea **N** **H** 893

Shoebury

London **A** ■ Benfleet

■ 892 Milton

Bath

Axbridge

Lyng

Langport

Wilton

Farnham 893

893 ■ Thorney Eashing

Lympne ■ 892

Shaftesbury

Winchester

Southampton
Porchester

Eorpeburnan

Burpham

Hastings

WESSEX

P Christchurch

Chichester

Lewes

Exeter

Lydford

Bridgeport

Wareham **M**

Halwell

F

D

B

C

G

E ✡ Pilton

The Conquest of the Danelaw

In just seven years, Wessex conquered much of the Danelaw, creating a unified kingdom of England

When Alfred the Great died in 899, Wessex was still on the defensive. His successor, Edward the Elder, was faced by a revolt by his cousin Aethelwold. In 903 the rebel persuaded the East Anglian Danes to invade Mercia and Wessex. Edward retaliated with a raid into the Danish-held Fens. Part of his army was defeated, but Aethelwold and the Danish King Eohric were killed. Peace returned until 909, when Edward despatched an army to attack the Northumbrian Danes. A Danish counter-attack, was defeated at Tettenhall in 910.

The power of the Kingdom of York was broken, and Edward's situation transformed. In co-operation with his sister Æthelflæd, the ruler of Mercia, he began a piecemeal but methodical conquest of the Danelaw south of the Humber. After the Danish king of East Anglia was killed in battle at Tempsford in 917, organized Danish resistance crumbled. Edward narrowly missed adding Northumbria to his kingdom. The Danes of Northumbria had submitted to Æthelflæd in 918, but she died before this coup could be followed up, and in the following year Ragnald, a Viking chief from Ireland, took control of York and the English-ruled Earldom of Northumbria.

The conquest of the Danelaw had taken just seven years. Alfred had left Edward with an efficient army which could remain in the field for months if need be, while the building of *burh* was an effective way of

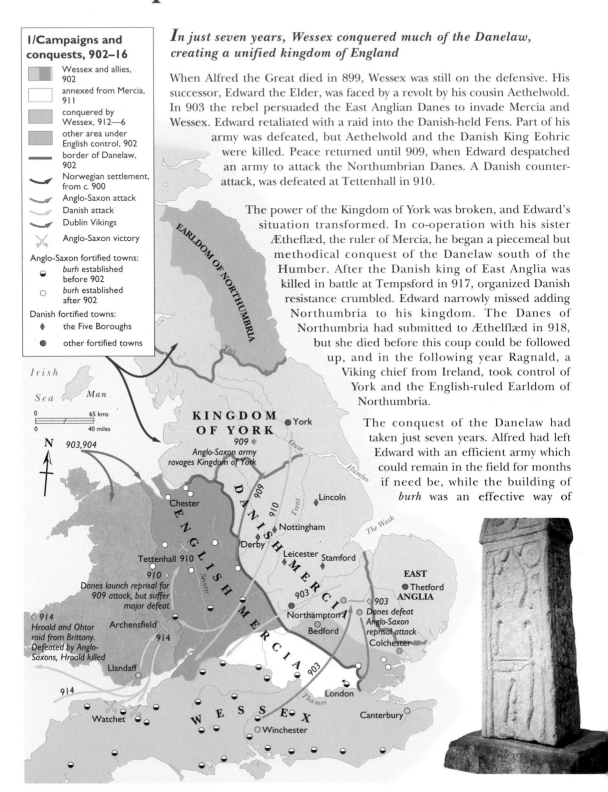

1/Campaigns and conquests, 902–16

- Wessex and allies, 902
- annexed from Mercia, 911
- conquered by Wessex, 912—6
- other area under English control, 902
- border of Danelaw, 902
- Norwegian settlement, from *c.* 900
- Anglo-Saxon attack
- Danish attack
- Dublin Vikings
- Anglo-Saxon victory

Anglo-Saxon fortified towns:
- *burh* established before 902
- *burh* established after 902

Danish fortified towns:
- the Five Boroughs
- other fortified towns

Irish Sea

Man

0 — 65 kms
0 — 40 miles

N

903, 904

EARLDOM OF NORTHUMBRIA

Tees

KINGDOM OF YORK
York

909
Anglo-Saxon army ravages Kingdom of York

Ouse

Humber

Chester

D A N I S H

909

910

Trent

Lincoln

Nottingham

Derby

Leicester   Stamford

The Wash

E N G L I S H   M E R C I A

Tettenhall 910

910
Danes launch reprisal for 909 attack, but suffer major defeat

Severn

903

EAST ANGLIA
Thetford

903
Danes defeat Anglo-Saxon reprisal attack

Northampton

Bedford

Colchester

914
Hroald and Ohtor raid from Brittany. Defeated by Anglo-Saxons, Hroald killed

Archensfield
914

Llandaff

914

903

London

Thames

Watchet

W E S S E X

Winchester

Canterbury

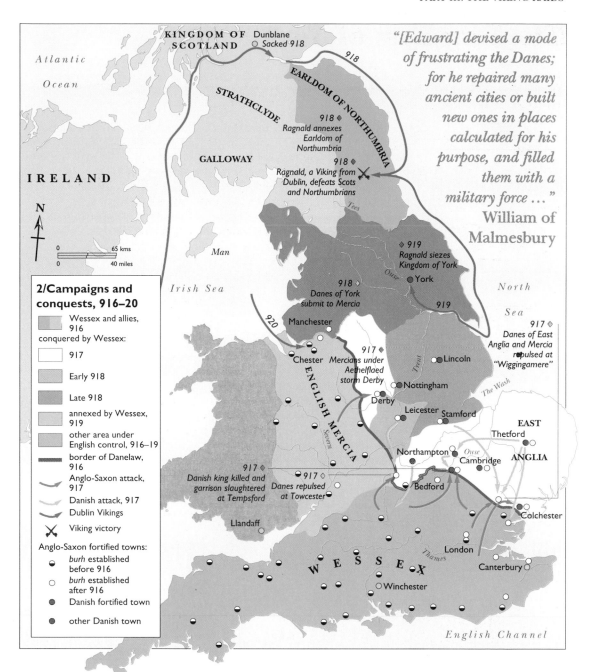

"[Edward] devised a mode of frustrating the Danes; for he repaired many ancient cities or built new ones in places calculated for his purpose, and filled them with a military force ..." William of Malmesbury

2/Campaigns and conquests, 916–20

Wessex and allies, 916

conquered by Wessex:

917

Early 918

Late 918

annexed by Wessex, 919

other area under English control, 916–19

border of Danelaw, 916

Anglo-Saxon attack, 917

Danish attack, 917

Dublin Vikings

✕ Viking victory

Anglo-Saxon fortified towns:

◗ *burh* established before 916

○ *burh* established after 916

● Danish fortified town

● other Danish town

KINGDOM OF SCOTLAND

Dunblane ○ Sacked 918

918

EARLDOM OF NORTHUMBRIA

STRATHCLYDE

918 ◆ Ragnald annexes Earldom of Northumbria

GALLOWAY

918 ◆ Ragnald, a Viking from Dublin, defeats Scots and Northumbrians

IRELAND

Atlantic Ocean

Man

Irish Sea

◆ 919 Ragnald siezes Kingdom of York

● York

918 ◆ Danes of York submit to Mercia

919

North Sea

917 ◆ Danes of East Anglia and Mercia repulsed at "Wiggingamere"

920

Manchester

Chester *Mercians under Aethelflaed storm Derby*

917 ◆

Lincoln

Nottingham

Derby

Leicester Stamford

EAST Thetford

ANGLIA

Cambridge

917 ◆ Danish king killed and garrison slaughtered at Tempsford

◆ 917 Danes repulsed at Towcester

Northampton

Ouse

Bedford

Colchester

Llandaff

London

Canterbury

W E S S E ✕ X

Winchester

English Channel

Left: *this 10th-century carving of a Danish warrior, from a stone cross in St Andrew's Church, Middleton in North Yorkshire, shows him wearing a Viking helmet and surrounded by the weapons of the period—a spear, round shield, sword and battle-axe. It may be a memorial to a Danelaw aristocrat who had been converted to Christianity.*

consolidating every advance. But the decisive factor was Danish weakness rather than English strength. Now that the Danes were settled, they had lost their main military advantage over the English, their mobility. They had crops to tend and homes to defend, and were less willing to spend months on campaign. Edward's achievement is often called the "reconquest" of the Danelaw, but it was, in effect, the West Saxon conquest of England. By no means all the English regarded Edward as a liberator—many fought with the Danes—and his campaigns ended with the formal annexation of English Mercia by the Kingdom of Wessex in 919.

The Kingdom of York

From 866 to 954 York was the centre of a Viking kingdom including most of the old kingdom of Northumbria south of the Tees.

Above: *Viking York flourished as a market for local goods and imports from Scandinavia, Ireland and Germany, and its kings struck large quantities of silver pennies. This coin of Olaf Guthfrithsson (c. 939–41, below) carries the pagan symbol of a raven with outstretched wings.*

After they took York in 866, the Danes at first ruled through English puppet kings, but in 876 Halfdan, one of the leaders of the Great Army, seized power. Halfdan—the first of many Vikings to dream of uniting York and Dublin—was killed in Ireland in 877. Little is known of his successors; some of them are known only from their coins. Danish control came under threat after an Irish victory over the Dublin Vikings in 902 brought an an influx of Irish-Norse settlers to northwest England. The death of three Danish kings at the battle of Tettenhall in 910 left the kingdom leaderless, and opened the way for the Irish-Norse Viking Ragnald to seize York in 919.

The Irish-Norse were never to establish themselves securely, however, and in 927 they were driven out by King Athelstan, who thereby completed the West Saxon dynasty's takeover of England. Olaf Guthfrithsson, King of Dublin, tried to regain York with the support of the Scots and Strathclyde Britons in 937, but was crushingly defeated by Athelstan at Brunanburh (location unknown, but probably near the Humber). In 939 Olaf was back. He conquered Northumbria and the Five Boroughs of the Danelaw in a lightning campaign, but his victory proved to be ephemeral; by 944, York was back in English hands. Erik Bloodaxe, an exiled king of Norway with a mighty reputation as a warrior, returned York to Viking control for the last time in 948. For the next six years he struggled for control with King Olaf Sihtricson of Dublin and the English King Eadred, but it was the Northumbrians themselves who drove him out of York to his death in an ambush on Stainmore in 954. Eadred, apparently unopposed, took control of Northumbria.

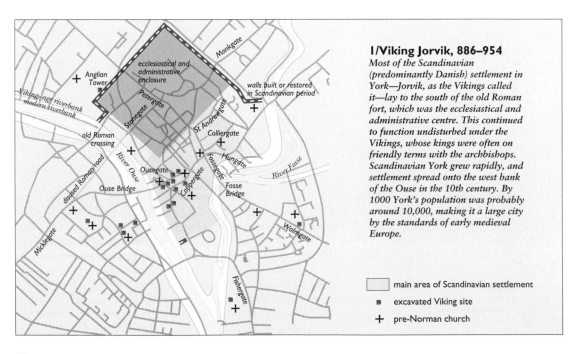

I/Viking Jorvik, 886–954

Most of the Scandinavian (predominantly Danish) settlement in York—Jorvik, as the Vikings called it—lay to the south of the old Roman fort, which was the ecclesiastical and administrative centre. This continued to function undisturbed under the Vikings, whose kings were often on friendly terms with the archbishops. Scandinavian York grew rapidly, and settlement spread onto the west bank of the Ouse in the 10th century. By 1000 York's population was probably around 10,000, making it a large city by the standards of early medieval Europe.

main area of Scandinavian settlement

excavated Viking site

pre-Norman church

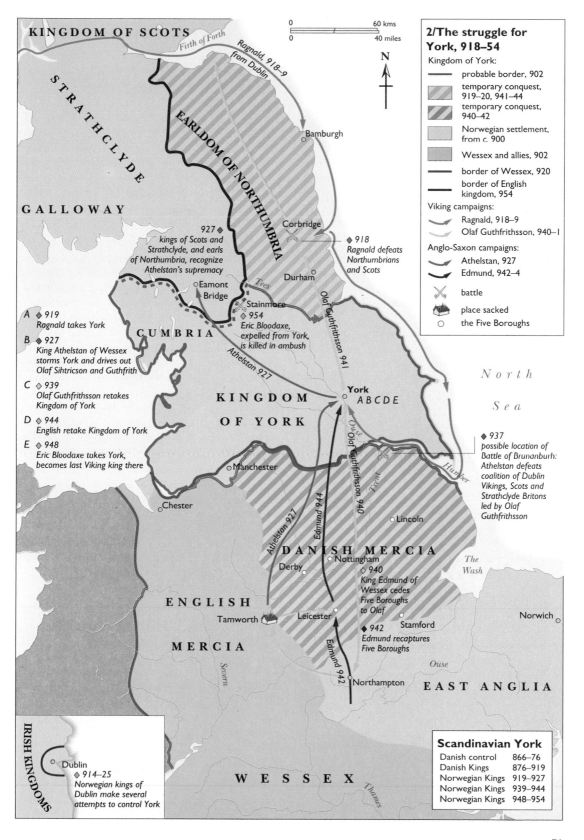

0   60 kms
0   40 miles

N

2/The struggle for York, 918–54

Kingdom of York:
— probable border, 902
▨ temporary conquest, 919–20, 941–44
▨ temporary conquest, 940–42
▨ Norwegian settlement, from *c.* 900
▨ Wessex and allies, 902
— border of Wessex, 920
— border of English kingdom, 954

Viking campaigns:
↘ Ragnald, 918–9
↘ Olaf Guthfrithsson, 940–1

Anglo-Saxon campaigns:
↘ Athelstan, 927
↘ Edmund, 942–4

✕ battle
🏰 place sacked
○ the Five Boroughs

KINGDOM OF SCOTS

Firth of Forth

Ragnald, 918–9 from Dublin

STRATHCLYDE

EARLDOM OF NORTHUMBRIA

Bamburgh

GALLOWAY

927 ◆
kings of Scots and Strathclyde, and earls of Northumbria, recognize Athelstan's supremacy

Corbridge ✕

◆ *918 Ragnald defeats Northumbrians and Scots*

Durham

○ Eamont Bridge

Tees

Stainmore ✕
◇ *954 Eric Bloodaxe, expelled from York, is killed in ambush*

CUMBRIA

Athelstan 927

Olaf Guthfrithsson 941

A ◆ *919 Ragnald takes York*

B ◆ *927 King Athelstan of Wessex storms York and drives out Olaf Sihtricson and Guthfrith*

C ◇ *939 Olaf Guthfrithsson retakes Kingdom of York*

D ◇ *944 English retake Kingdom of York*

E ◆ *948 Eric Bloodaxe takes York, becomes last Viking king there*

KINGDOM OF YORK

York
A B C D E

Ouse
Olaf Guthfrithsson 940

North Sea

◆ *937 possible location of Battle of Brunanburh: Athelstan defeats coalition of Dublin Vikings, Scots and Strathclyde Britons led by Olaf Guthfrithsson*

○ Manchester

○ Chester

Trent
Humber

Lincoln ○

DANISH MERCIA

Athelstan 927

Edmund 944

○ Nottingham
◇ *940 King Edmund of Wessex cedes Five Boroughs to Olaf*

Derby ○

The Wash

ENGLISH

Tamworth 🏰

Leicester ○

◆ *942 Edmund recaptures Five Boroughs*

Stamford ○

Norwich ○

MERCIA

Severn

Edmund 942

Northampton ○

Ouse

EAST ANGLIA

WESSEX

Thames

IRISH KINGDOMS

○ Dublin
◇ *914–25 Norwegian kings of Dublin make several attempts to control York*

Scandinavian York

Danish control	866–76
Danish Kings	876–919
Norwegian Kings	919–927
Norwegian Kings	939–944
Norwegian Kings	948–954

Vikings in Ireland I

Vikings raided the coast of Ireland, sailed up rivers to strike deep inland and established a permanent settlement at Dublin.

Ireland's Viking age began with a raid on a church on Lambey Island near Dublin in 795. Viking activity developed in a similar way to that in Britain and Francia. The first phase, which lasted until around 830, involved small fleets in uncoordinated attacks on targets—primarily monasteries—within 20 miles of the coast. In the 830s raiding became much more frequent, and the fleets larger. Inland areas became vulnerable as the Viking fleets began to sail up navigable rivers such as the Shannon, sacking the monastery at Clonmacnoise in 836, and then into Lough Erne and Lough Neagh.

Early 9th-century Ireland was divided into five competing high kingdoms, but the high kings had little control over their quarrelsome sub-kings, so there was no coordinated response to the raids. By 840 the Vikings had become a permanent presence, building fortified camps, the most important of which was at Dublin. Around this time the shadowy warlord Turgeis provides the first evidence that Viking ambitions now extended beyond plunder to conquest and political control. Once the Vikings began to develop permanent settlements, they became more vulnerable to counter-attack, and Irish resistance became more effective. In 847 the Vikings suffered four major defeats, after which many of them moved to Francia.

The first raiders and settlers had been Norwegians, but in 851 the Danes won control of Dublin, only to be expelled two years later by Olaf the White, a son of a Norwegian king. Olaf made himself king of Dublin, and under him the Vikings began to be drawn into Irish political life, alternately fighting and allying with their neighbours. When Olaf's successor Ivar died in 873, the Dublin kingdom entered a period of political instability. Many Vikings left Ireland to raid in England or Francia or settle in Iceland, and for the next 40 years Ireland saw little Viking activity.

Above: this small human figure, an enamelled mount from a bronze bowl, was found in a Viking grave in Scandinavia. It is typical of the many fine pieces of Irish craftsmanship pillaged by the Vikings. The 9th century saw the end of the "golden age" of early Christian Irish civilization, which produced treasures such as the high crosses, the Book of Kells and the Ardagh chalice.

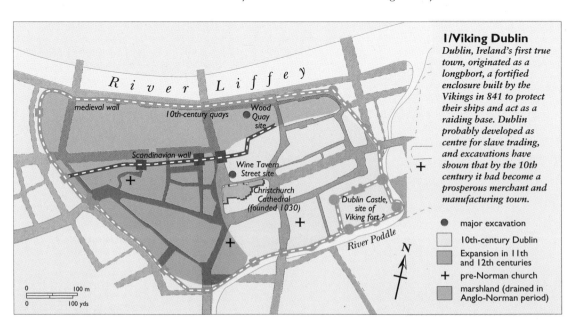

I/Viking Dublin

Dublin, Ireland's first true town, originated as a longphort, a fortified enclosure built by the Vikings in 841 to protect their ships and act as a raiding base. Dublin probably developed as centre for slave trading, and excavations have shown that by the 10th century it had become a prosperous merchant and manufacturing town.

- ● major excavation
- ☐ 10th-century Dublin
- ☐ Expansion in 11th and 12th centuries
- + pre-Norman church
- ☐ marshland (drained in Anglo-Norman period)

River Liffey

medieval wall
10th-century quays
Wood Quay site
Scandinavian wall
Wine Tavern Street site
Christchurch Cathedral (founded 1030)
Dublin Castle, site of Viking fort ?
River Poddle

N

0 — 100 m
0 — 100 yds

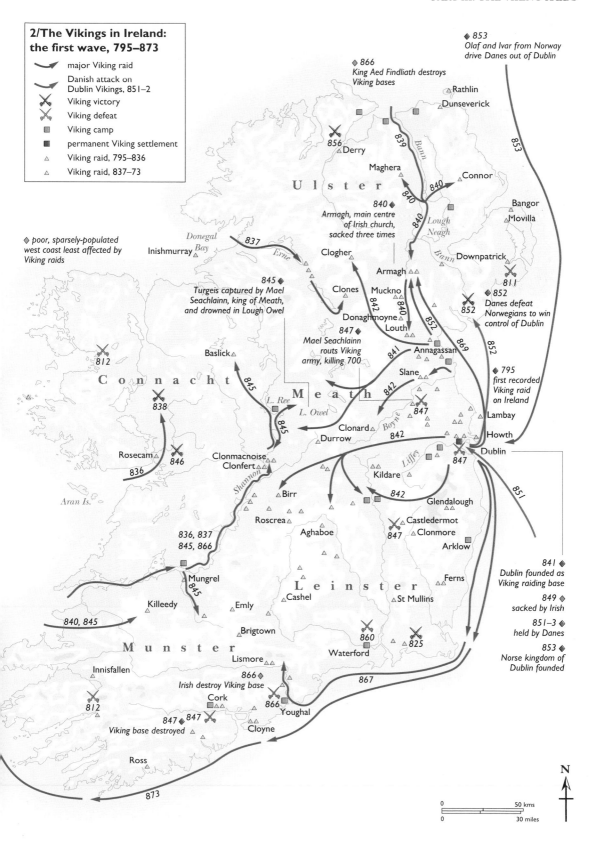

2/The Vikings in Ireland: the first wave, 795–873

- ⟶ major Viking raid
- ⟶ Danish attack on Dublin Vikings, 851–2
- ✗ Viking victory
- ✗ Viking defeat
- ◻ Viking camp
- ◼ permanent Viking settlement
- △ Viking raid, 795–836
- △ Viking raid, 837–73

853
Olaf and Ivar from Norway drive Danes out of Dublin

866
King Aed Findliath destroys Viking bases

Rathlin
Dunseverick

856
Derry

Maghera

Connor

Bangor
Movilla

U l s t e r

840
Armagh, main centre of Irish church, sacked three times

Lough Neagh

Downpatrick

811

◆ *poor, sparsely-populated west coast least affected by Viking raids*

Donegal Bay
Inishmurray

837

Erne

Clogher

Armagh

852
Danes defeat Norwegians to win control of Dublin

845 ◆
Turgeis captured by Mael Seachlainn, king of Meath, and drowned in Lough Owel

Clones
Clonfert

Muckno

842

840

Donaghmoyne

Louth

847 ◆
Mael Seachlainn routs Viking army, killing 700

Annagassan

869

852

795
first recorded Viking raid on Ireland

812

C o n n a c h t

838

Baslick

845

L. Ree

M e a t h

L. Owel

841

Slane

842

847

Lambay

Howth

Rosecam

846

836

Clonmacnoise
Clonfert

Shannon

Clonard
Durrow

Boyne

842

Kildare

842

Glendalough

Dublin

847

851

841 ◆
Dublin founded as Viking raiding base

Aran Is.

Birr

Roscrea

Aghaboe

Castledermot

847

Clonmore

Arklow

849 ◆
sacked by Irish

**836, 837
845, 866**

Mungrel

845

Killeedy

Emly

L e i n s t e r

Cashel

St Mullins

Ferns

851–3 ◆
held by Danes

840, 845

Brigtown

860

825

853 ◆
Norse kingdom of Dublin founded

M u n s t e r

Lismore

Waterford

Innisfallen

866
Irish destroy Viking base

Cork

866

Youghal

867

812

847 ◆ **847**
Viking base destroyed

Cloyne

Ross

873

N

0 ———— 50 kms
0 ———— 30 miles

Vikings in Ireland II

"Brodir... ran from the woods and burst through the wall of shields, and hacked at the king. The boy Tadk threw up an arm to protect King Brian, but the sword cut off the arm and the king's head. The king's blood spilled over the stump of the boy's arm, and the wound healed at once."
the death of Brian Boru, from *Njal's Saga*

***T**he "Forty Years' Rest" was followed by renewed raiding but gradually the Vikings were assimilated into the Irish population.*

The long respite from Viking raids which Ireland enjoyed between 874 and 914 became known as the "Forty Years' Rest". Many Vikings had moved to England or Francia where raiding was now reaching its peak; those who remained suffered a series of defeats culminating with their expulsion from Dublin in 902. But as the opportunities for raiding in England and Francia declined, the Vikings turned their attention to Ireland again. Within a few years the Vikings were re-established in strength at Dublin, Wexford, Waterford and Limerick, and were once again raiding deep inland along Ireland's navigable rivers. Ireland also experienced a great deal of small scale coastal raiding by Vikings settled in the Hebrides and northern isles, which continued into the 12th century.

The Vikings made no lasting territorial conquests or extensive settlements. The Dublin Vikings were frequently diverted by their ambitions to rule York, while the Irish-Norse towns were often at odds with each other. Irish resistance was often highly effective and it was only Ireland's disunity that enabled the Viking enclaves to survive. Tradition has it that Ireland's Viking age ended at the battle of Clontarf in 1014, when Brian Boru, the king of Munster, defeated an alliance between Leinster and the Dublin Vikings, though he himself was killed in the fighting. In reality, it ended more with a whimper than a bang. Under constant pressure from the kings of Munster in the south and the kings of Meath in the north, the power of the Irish-Norse was in sharp decline by the late 10th century. Though the native kingdoms often sought them as allies because of their fighting qualities, they had little influence in their own right: several times before 1000 the Dublin Vikings had been forced to pay tribute to Irish kings as the price of keeping their independence. By this time the Irish-Norse were beginning to lose their Viking identity through conversion to Christianity, intermarriage with the Irish and adoption of the Gaelic language; the Irish now knew them as the "Ostmen" (men of the east) to distinguish them from the Scandinavians.

Left: *in response to the Viking raids of the 10th century, the Irish built a series of church belltowers which could also serve as lookout posts and refuges, like this one on the monastic island of Devenish in Lough Erne.*

Right: *although the Vikings had little long-term influence in Ireland, Scandinavian styles did find their way into Irish art. The Cross of Cong was made around 1123, long after the Irish Vikings had lost their independence but its decoration still shows a strong influence of the late Norse Urnes style.*

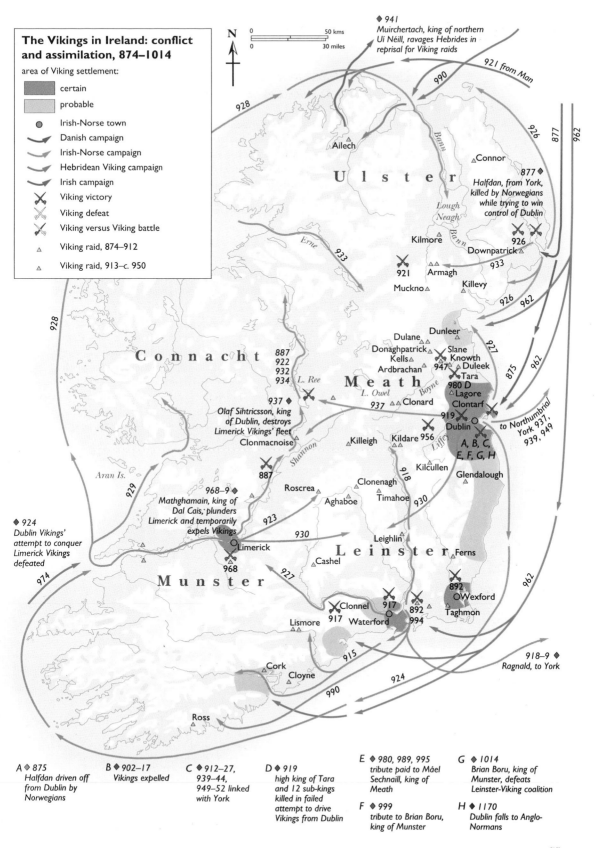

The Vikings in Ireland: conflict and assimilation, 874–1014

area of Viking settlement:

- certain
- probable
- Irish-Norse town
- Danish campaign
- Irish-Norse campaign
- Hebridean Viking campaign
- Irish campaign
- Viking victory
- Viking defeat
- Viking versus Viking battle
- Viking raid, 874–912
- Viking raid, 913–c. 950

N

50 kms
30 miles

*941
Muirchertach, king of northern
Uí Néill, ravages Hebrides in
reprisal for Viking raids*

921 from Man

928

990

926

877

962

U l s t e r

Ailech

Connor

877
*Halfdan, from York,
killed by Norwegians
while trying to win
control of Dublin*

Bann

Lough
Neagh

Kilmore

Downpatrick

Erne

933

921

Armagh

Muckno

Killevy

926

933

926

962

C o n n a c h t

928

887
922
932
934 L. Ree

937
*Olaf Sihtricsson, king
of Dublin, destroys
Limerick Vikings' fleet*

Clonmacnoise

887

929

Aran Is.

M u n s t e r

924
*Dublin Vikings'
attempt to conquer
Limerick Vikings
defeated*

974

968–9
*Mathghamain, king of
Dal Cais, plunders
Limerick and temporarily
expels Vikings*

Limerick

968

923

927

930

Dulane

Donaghpatrick
Kells
Ardbrachan

Dunleer

Slane
Knowth
Duleek

947

M e a t h

L. Owel
L. Ree

937

Clonard

Tara

980 D
Lagore
Clontarf

919
Dublin

956

A, B, C,
E, F, G, H

Boyne

Killeigh

Kildare

Kilcullen

Glendalough

Roscrea

Clonenagh
Aghaboe
Timahoe

930

918

Leighlin

L e i n s t e r

Ferns

Cashel

927

Clonmel

917
917
Waterford

892
994

Taghmon

Wexford

892

Lismore

915

Cork
Cloyne

990

924

Ross

875
*Halfdan driven off
from Dublin by
Norwegians*

927

875

962

to Northumbria/
York 937,
939, 949

918–9
Ragnald, to York

A ◆ 875
Halfdan driven off
from Dublin by
Norwegians

B ◆ 902–17
Vikings expelled

C ◆ 912–27,
939–44,
949–52 linked
with York

D ◆ 919
high king of Tara
and 12 sub-kings
killed in failed
attempt to drive
Vikings from Dublin

E ◆ 980, 989, 995
tribute paid to Máel
Sechnaill, king of
Meath

F ◆ 999
tribute to Brian Boru,
king of Munster

G ◆ 1014
Brian Boru, king of
Munster, defeats
Leinster-Viking coalition

H ◆ 1170
Dublin falls to Anglo-
Normans

The Vikings in Scotland

Viking raids on monasteries were followed by permanent settlements in the Scottish islands and along the coast.

"They plundered the Hebrides, reaching the Barra Isles, where a king called Kjarval ruled ... There was a fierce battle ... After many had fallen on both sides, the battle ended with the king taking flight with a single ship ..."
Grettir's Saga

The earliest recorded Viking activity in Scotland was an attack on the monastery of Colmcille on Iona in 795. Over the next 50 years raids continued unabated around the western coasts. By the mid-9th century, however, the emphasis had shifted from raiding to settlement. Very little is known about the settlement process, but the first settlements probably began as raiding bases early in the century. By 900, settlers—mostly Norwegians—were well established in the islands and along the coast from Galloway to the Moray Firth. In Orkney and Shetland the native Celts were completely submerged by the newcomers, but in the Hebrides and the southwest they were soon intermarrying with the Norse to produce a hybrid people known to the Irish as the Gall-Gaedhil ("foreign Gael"), from which Galloway gets its name. One result of Celtic influence was that many of the settlers adopted Christianity before 900.

The political organization of the settlements is uncertain but, as later in Iceland, they were probably made under aristocratic leaders such as Ketil Flatnose who ruled in the Hebrides from around 840 to 880. Towards the end of the 9th century, the Norwegian Vestfold kings extended their authority over Orkney, establishing an earldom under loose royal control. They also claimed sovereignty over the Hebrides, but it would be 200 years before their authority there was anything more than theoretical. The Orkney earldom soon expanded, taking control of most of the Scandinavian settled areas of Scotland by the reign of Earl Sigurd the Stout (*c.* 985–1014).

The most important effect that the Vikings had on Scotland in this period was to break the existing power structures. In 800, Scotland was divided between four ethnic groups: the Picts of the Highlands, the Scots of Dalriada, the Britons of Strathclyde and the Anglo-Saxons of Northumbria. All four suffered from Viking attacks, but the Scots seem to have been weakened less than their neighbours. Turning circumstances to their advantage, they overran the Picts in 844, the Strathclyde Britons in the 920s and Lothian in 973, to create the kingdom of Scotland.

Below: *St Columba's Abbey on the island of Iona was one of the first places in Scotland attacked by the Vikings. As the Norse settlers of the isles converted by Christianity, Viking rulers became patrons —rather than plunderers—of the abbey. By the 11th century it had become the burial place of the Norse kings of Man and the Isles.*

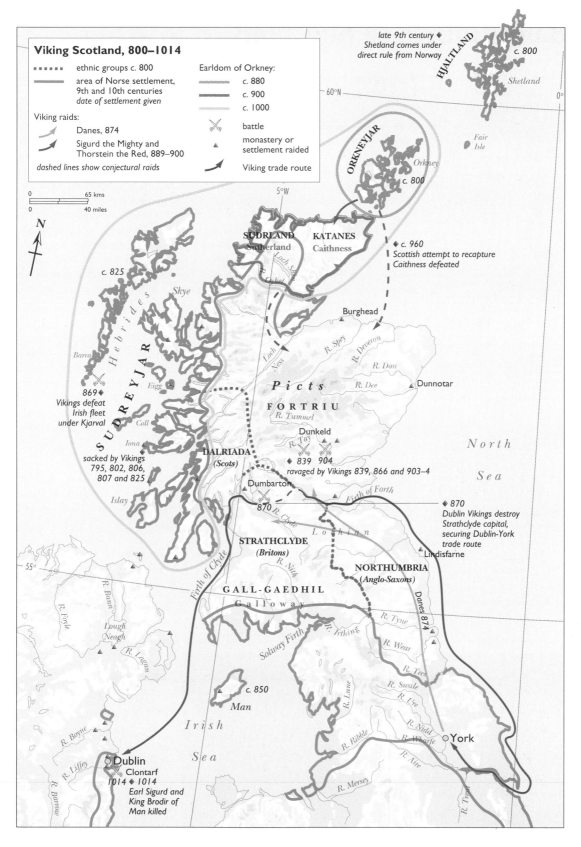

Viking Scotland, 800–1014

- ▪▪▪▪▪ ethnic groups c. 800
- ▬▬▬▬ area of Norse settlement, 9th and 10th centuries date of settlement given

Viking raids:

- ↗ Danes, 874
- ➜ Sigurd the Mighty and Thorstein the Red, 889–900

dashed lines show conjectural raids

Earldom of Orkney:
- ▬▬▬ c. 880
- ▬▬▬ c. 900
- ▬▬▬ c. 1000

- ⚔ battle
- ▲ monastery or settlement raided
- ➤ Viking trade route

0 ___ 65 kms
0 ___ 40 miles

N

late 9th century ◆
Shetland comes under
direct rule from Norway

HJALTLAND
c. 800
Shetland

60°N   0°

*Fair
Isle*

ORKNEYJAR
Orkney
c. 800

5°W

SUDRLAND
Sutherland   KATANES
Caithness

◆ c. 960
Scottish attempt to recapture
Caithness defeated

c. 825

Skye

Burghead

Loch Shin

R. Oykel

Loch Ness

R. Spey
R. Deveron

R. Don

R. Dee   ▪ Dunnotar

Barra

P i c t s

869 ◆
Vikings defeat
Irish fleet
under Kjarval

Eigg

FORTRIU
R. Tummel

Coll

Dunkeld
R. Tay

Iona ▲
sacked by Vikings
795, 802, 806,
807 and 825

DALRIADA
(Scots)

◆ 839 904
ravaged by Vikings 839, 866 and 903–4

Islay

North

Sea

Dumbarton

870 R. Clyde

◆ 870
Dublin Vikings destroy
Strathclyde capital,
securing Dublin-York
trade route

55°

STRATHCLYDE
(Britons)

L o t h i a n

Firth of Forth

R. Nith   Lindisfarne ▲

GALL-GAEDHIL
G a l l o w a y

NORTHUMBRIA
(Anglo-Saxons)

R. Bann

R. Foyle

*Lough
Neagh*

R. Lagan

Solway Firth

R. Irthing

R. Tyne   Danes 874

R. Wear

R. Tees

R. Lune

R. Swale

R. Ure

R. Nidd

R. Ribble   R. Wharfe

c. 850
Man

Irish

R. Boyne

◎ Dublin
Clontarf
1014 ◆ 1014
Earl Sigurd and
King Brodir of
Man killed

R. Liffey

R. Barrow

Sea

R. Aire

R. Mersey

R. Trent

◎ York

77

Scandinavian Place Names in Britain

Above: *placenames of Norse origin predominate in much of northwest England. However the survival of Anglo-Saxon placenames such as Kaber (ca-beorg = "jackdaw hill") alongside names of pure Norse origin such as Keld ("spring") and Thwaite ("clearing") show that the native inhabitants were not driven out by the new settlers.*

Below: *this sundial in the porch of St Gregory's Minster at Kirkdale in Yorkshire shows the Norse settlers becoming assimilated into the Anglo-Saxon population. A man with a Scandinavian name has restored a Christian church and recorded the fact in Anglo-Saxon: "Orm, son of Gamal, acquired the church of St Gregory when it was tumbled and ruined, and had it rebuilt from the ground in honour of Christ and St Gregory" during the earldom of Tostig (1055–65).*

Placenames are the most important source of evidence about the extent of Viking settlement in Britain and Ireland.

If we had to rely only on archaeological evidence, such as burials, stone-carvings or settlements, the picture would be much less complete. This is especially true in England, where Scandinavian settlements have proved very difficult to identify. Though many Scandinavian placenames date from after the Viking age, their distribution gives a broad indication of the density of Scandinavian settlement. In Orkney, Shetland and Caithness, almost all placenames are of Scandinavian character. Scandinavian placenames are also common in the Isle of Man, Cumbria, Yorkshire and the East Midlands; in East Anglia, the Hebrides and Galloway; and, to a lesser extent, along the coasts of northwest Scotland, Lancashire, Cheshire and South Wales. There are few Scandinavian placenames in England south of the 9th-century border of the Danelaw, and they are absent even from many areas north of it.

Despite the Vikings' long involvement in Ireland, there are few Scandinavian placenames there, mirroring the lack of literary and archaeological evidence for Scandinavian settlement outside their coastal bases. A scattering of prominent coastal features, especially around the Irish Sea, have Scandinavian names—a sign of the Scandinavian domination of these waters during the Viking age. In general, Norwegian placename elements are commonest in northwest England, Man and Scotland, and Danish elements in eastern England. The most characteristic Danish placename elements are *-by,* as in Thurkleby ("Thurkil's farmstead"), and *-thorpe* as in Kettlethorpe ("Ketil's outlying farm"). Hybrid names incorporating a Danish personal name and the English element *-tun,* as in Grimston ("Grim's village"), are also common in the Danelaw. Typical Norwegian placename elements found in the northern isles are *-stathir,* found in Grimista ("Grim's place"), and *-bólstadr,* as in Isbister ("eastern farm"). The Norwegian *-thveit* in, Brackenthwaite ("bracken clearing"), is common in Cumbria and Dumfries. Common Scandinavian elements in coastal placenames are *-ey* (island), *-holm* (islet), *-wick* (bay) and *-ford* (fjord).

Man

Mull, Jura & Islay

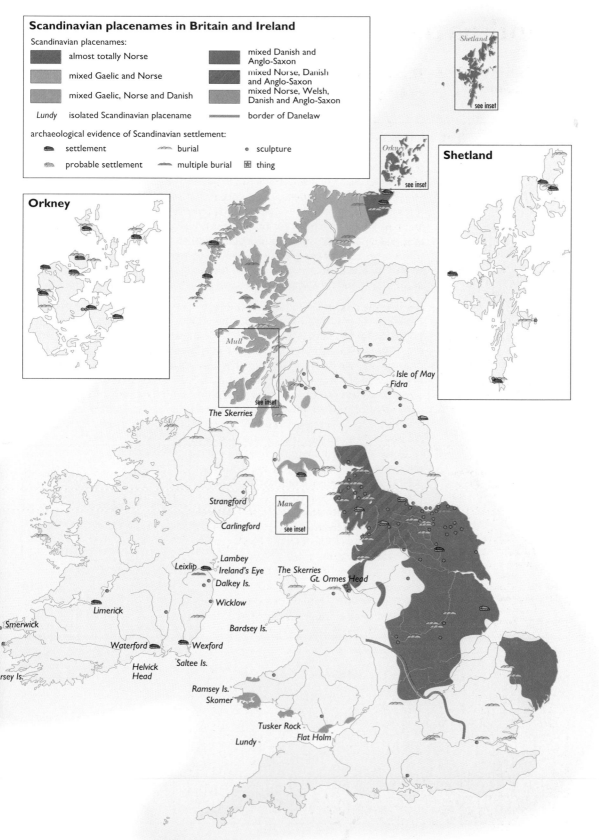

Scandinavian placenames in Britain and Ireland

Scandinavian placenames:

almost totally Norse

mixed Gaelic and Norse

mixed Gaelic, Norse and Danish

mixed Danish and Anglo-Saxon

mixed Norse, Danish and Anglo-Saxon

mixed Norse, Welsh, Danish and Anglo-Saxon

Lundy isolated Scandinavian placename

border of Danelaw

archaeological evidence of Scandinavian settlement:

settlement

probable settlement

burial

multiple burial

sculpture

thing

Shetland

Orkney

Shetland

Orkney

see inset

Mull

see inset

The Skerries

Isle of May

Fidra

Strangford

Carlingford

Man

see inset

Lambey

Ireland's Eye

Dalkey Is.

Wicklow

The Skerries

Gt. Ormes Head

Leixlip

Limerick

Bardsey Is.

Smerwick

Waterford

Wexford

Saltee Is.

Helvick Head

ursey Is.

Ramsey Is.

Skomer

Tusker Rock

Flat Holm

Lundy

The Duchy of Normandy

Rollo's Vikings, allowed to settle in Normandy as a defence against other raiders, rapidly adopted a French, Christian identity.

In 892, most of the Vikings on the Seine crossed the Channel to raid in England, and those who remained began to settle down. Their last major raid—on Chartres in 911—was defeated, and their leader Rollo made a peace agreement with the Frankish King Charles the Simple. In return for his homage and conversion to Christianity, Rollo was made count of Rouen (the rulers of Normandy did not use the title "duke" before 1006). Charles' intention was that Rollo would prevent any other Vikings sailing down the Seine to attack his kingdom. In this respect, the agreement was a great success and, apart from some border troubles, the Viking threat to the Seine valley was permanently ended. Rollo was granted further lands around Bayeux in 924 and his successor William Longsword acquired the Cotentin peninsula in 933, but attempts to expand eastwards were defeated.

Normandy—from Normannia, or "Northman's Land"—owes its name to the Vikings, but their long-term influence was slight. Placename evidence points to fairly dense Scandinavian (mainly Danish) settlement in coastal areas, but elsewhere it was very sparse: the Scandinavians were clearly a minority in Normandy as a whole. The settlers have left little archaeological evidence of their presence, indicating that they quickly adopted Frankish material culture and burial practices. Some newly arrived settlers started a brief pagan revival around 942, but most of the earlier settlers had already converted by this stage. Economic ties with the north, never strong, were abandoned by the late 10th century. Scandinavian speech probably survived until the early 11th century. The last vestige of Scandinavian cultural influence was the presence of a Norwegian poet at the ducal court in 1025. Well before 1066, Normandy had become, administratively, culturally and linguistically, a French principality.

Above: one of *a pair of Scandinavian fibulae, or clothes fasteners, found in a Viking grave at Pîtres in Normandy.*

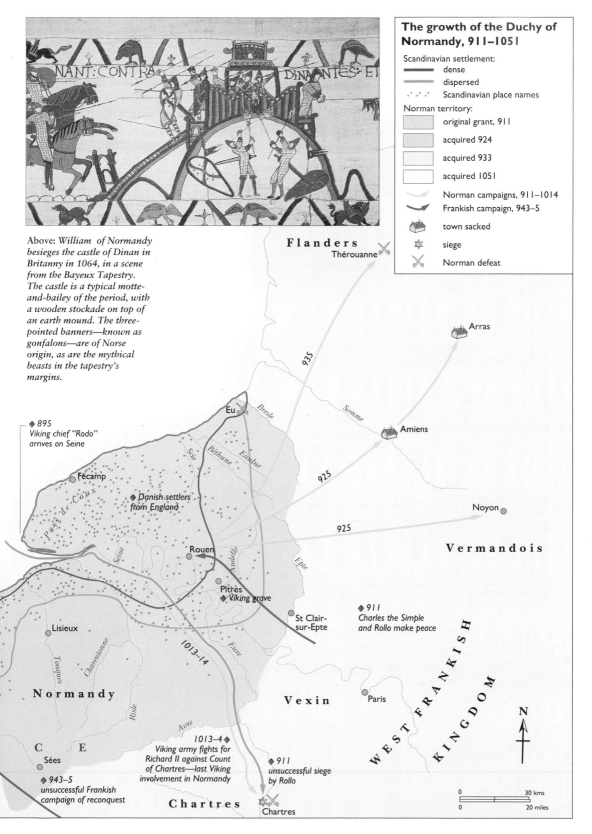

Above: *William of Normandy besieges the castle of Dinan in Britanny in 1064, in a scene from the Bayeux Tapestry. The castle is a typical motte-and-bailey of the period, with a wooden stockade on top of an earth mound. The three-pointed banners—known as gonfalons—are of Norse origin, as are the mythical beasts in the tapestry's margins.*

The growth of the Duchy of Normandy, 911–1051

Scandinavian settlement:
— dense
— dispersed
· · · Scandinavian place names

Norman territory:
  original grant, 911
  acquired 924
  acquired 933
  acquired 1051

Norman campaigns, 911–1014
Frankish campaign, 943–5
town sacked
siege
Norman defeat

Flanders

Thérouanne

935

Arras

Eu

Bresle

Somme

Amiens

◆ 895
Viking chief "Rodo" arrives on Seine

Saie

Béthune

Eaulne

Fécamp

925

Noyon

Pays de Caux

◆ *Danish settlers from England*

Seine

Rouen

Andelle

Epte

925

Vermandois

Pitres
◆ *Viking grave*

St Clair-sur-Epte

◆ 911
Charles the Simple and Rollo make peace

Lisieux

1013–14

Eure

W E S T   F R A N K I S H   K I N G D O M

Charentonne

Touques

Normandy

Risle

Vexin

Paris

Avre

N C E

Sées

◆ 1013–4
Viking army fights for Richard II against Count of Chartres—last Viking involvement in Normandy

◆ 911
unsuccessful siege by Rollo

N

◆ 943–5
unsuccessful Frankish campaign of reconquest

Chartres

Chartres

0   30 kms
0   20 miles

The Vikings in Brittany

Blocked out of the Seine by the Normans, the Vikings invaded Brittany and drove its nobles into exile.

For most of the 9th century, Britanny escaped relatively lightly from Viking attacks; although it suffered its share of coastal raids, the region was peripheral to the Vikings' main interests. The worst attacks were probably in 847 and 888, when parts of Brittany were briefly occupied, but a series of Breton victories 888–91 won the region a 20-year respite. In many ways the Vikings were more of a help than a hinderance to the Bretons in this period. The Frankish emperors were too preoccupied with internal problems and Viking attacks to prevent the Bretons expanding to the south and west, and were obliged to recognize Brittany's independence. The Vikings proved useful allies; a joint Breton-Viking army attacked Le Mans in 865.

But in the 10th century, the situation changed. The settlement of Rollo and his followers in Normandy in 911 closed the Seine to Viking raids, and in England the Danes were being pushed onto the defensive. Only Brittany and Ireland remained open to attack, and from 912 the raids intensified. Most coastal monasteries were abandoned as their terrified monks fled with their relics and manuscripts. By 919 Brittany's defences had completely collapsed: the nobility fled to Francia and England, and the Vikings under Rognvald conquered the whole country, making their capital at Nantes. The conquest seems to have been a purely military takeover: there is no evidence of any settlement nor, apparently, did the Vikings engage in trade. Nantes, whose position at the mouth of the Loire should have enabled it to become a flourishing trade centre like York or Dublin, was semi-derelict when the Bretons recaptured it.

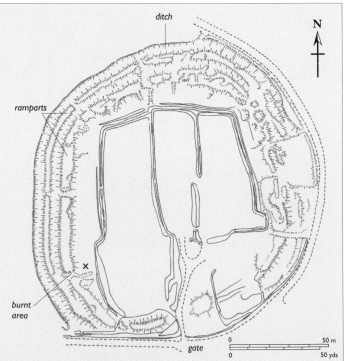

2/The fort at Camp de Péran

The fort at Camp de Péran was either built or occupied by the Vikings in the early 10th century; weapons and pottery of the period have been found there, as well as a coin from York. Its shape and construction are similiar to that of the round forts of Denmark (▶ page 84). Its earthen ramparts, some 12 feet (4 metres) high, would have been topped by a wooden stockade. The fort was destroyed by fire some time during the 930s, possibly during Alan Barbetorte's invasion. In places the heat was so intense that the clay ramparts have become vitrified.

✕ 10th-century coin from York

ditch

N

ramparts

burnt
area

gate

0   50 m
0   50 yds

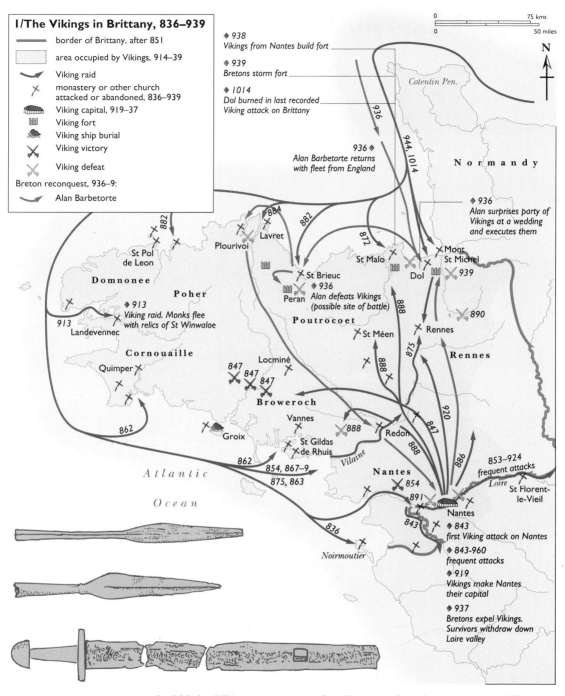

I/The Vikings in Brittany, 836–939

- border of Brittany, after 851
- area occupied by Vikings, 914–39
- Viking raid
- monastery or other church attacked or abandoned, 836–939
- Viking capital, 919–37
- Viking fort
- Viking ship burial
- Viking victory
- Viking defeat

Breton reconquest, 936–9:
- Alan Barbetorte

◆ *938*
Vikings from Nantes build fort

◆ *939*
Bretons storm fort

◆ *1014*
Dol burned in last recorded Viking attack on Brittany

Cotentin Pen.

936 ◆
Alan Barbetorte returns with fleet from England

N o r m a n d y

◆ *936*
Alan surprises party of Vikings at a wedding and executes them

St Pol de Leon

D o m n o n e e

Plourivoi Lavret

882

884

882

872

P o h e r

St Malo

Mont St Michel

Dol

939

◆ *913*
Viking raid. Monks flee with relics of St Winwaloe

913 Landevennec

St Brieuc

Peran

◆ *936*
Alan defeats Vikings (possible site of battle)

P o u t r o c o e t

888

890

C o r n o u a i l l e

St Méen

Rennes

Quimper

R e n n e s

Locminé

847 847 847

B r o w e r o c h

Vannes

888

Redon

875

888

920

847

886

A t l a n t i c

O c e a n

862

Groix

St Gildas de Rhuis

Vilaine

N a n t e s

854

891

843

853–924
frequent attacks

Loire

St Florent-le-Vieil

862

854, 867–9
875, 863

Nantes

◆ *843*
first Viking attack on Nantes

836

Noirmoutier

◆ *843-960*
frequent attacks

◆ *919*
Vikings make Nantes their capital

◆ *937*
Bretons expel Vikings. Survivors withdraw down Loire valley

Above: *three of the weapons found in the Viking fort at Camp de Péran—a longsword with a pattern-welded blade, and two iron spearheads.*

In 931 the Vikings concentrated at Nantes to launch an invasion of Francia. The Bretons saw their chance and rebelled. Though the rebellion was put down the weakness of the Vikings' position was exposed. This encouraged Alan Barbetorte ("twisted-beard"), an exile in England, to lead an invasion of Brittany in 936. Nantes was retaken after a fierce battle in 937 and the last Vikings were expelled from their fort at Trans near Dol in 939. The effect of the Viking occupation was disastrous for Breton independence, however. The authority of the dukes never fully recovered, and by the 11th century Brittany had become a satellite of Normandy.

The Viking Warrior

Richly decorated weapons and lavish burials proclaimed the status of Viking warriors; bonded by loyalty and pride, they were the elite of their society.

Right: *this carved wooden head on the Oseberg cart (c. 800) shows the fierce Viking warrior of legend. The cart is part of the rich assemblage of grave goods of a Viking queen in the Oseberg ship burial from Norway.*

Very little is known about the organization of the Viking armies that ravaged western Europe. The basic unit was the *lið*, a king's or chieftain's private retinue of warriors. The warriors of the *lið* formed a *félag* or fellowship, bonded together by mutual loyalty. Discipline was probably maintained mainly by the individual warrior's fear of dishonour if he abandoned his leader and companions in battle: ideally a warrior should follow his leader to his death if necessary. A Viking army was simply a group of *lið* which had come together for a common purpose. When a campaign was over the army dispersed into its respective fellowships to settle, go home or join another army somewhere else. Local defence within Scandinavia was provided for by a levy system which required all able-bodied men to bear arms in an emergency. The local chieftain's *lið* probably provided the backbone of the levies. In battle, Viking warriors expected their kings or chieftains to lead from the front under their standards. In an age of primitive battlefield communications, the standard showed warriors the direction of advance and provided a rallying point in dire emergency. The most feared Viking warriors were the berserkers, devotees of the war god Odin. Their name is probably derived from the bearskin shirts they wore. Berserkers worked themselves into a trance-like frenzy before battle which apparently left them immune to the pain of wounds.

Vikings did not go out of their way to seek battle, but if there was no alternative the usual tactic was to form a defensive shield wall to meet the enemy attack. Two forces could be locked in battle for hours, shield wall to shield wall: the decisive moment came when one force lost its nerve and tried to withdraw, or when its shield wall was broken. Casualties could be very one-sided, as the victors could inflict great slaughter on a fleeing enemy without much risk to themselves. Despite the Vikings' skill as navigators, sea battles were rare; when they did occur, the main tactic was to board the enemy ship and clear its decks by hand-to-hand fighting.

The most favoured weapon in Denmark and Norway was the double-edged longsword, which was used for hacking at the enemy rather than thrusting. Frankish swords were prized for their quality, but Scandinavian smiths were also highly skilled, and their finest swords had a pattern-welded core to give greater strength and flexibility. Axes are the weapon with which the Vikings are most often associated, and these were often used as a cheaper alternative to a sword. In Sweden the most common weapon was the spear, with a pattern-welded socketed blade up to 2 feet (60 cm) long mounted on an

ash shaft 6–9 feet (2–3 m) long. The sockets of the finest quality spears were inlaid with patterns in silver. Bows and arrows and fighting knives were also used. The most important defensive weapon was the circular shield. Usually these were made of wood with iron bands to strengthen the rim and an iron boss which held the grip and could be used also as a knuckle-duster. Shields were about 3 feet (1 m) in diameter to protect the whole body from the neck to the thighs. Towards the end of the Viking age, the round shield was superseded by the kite-shaped shield. Those who could afford them wore chain mail coats and metal helmets (usually fitted with face guards), but most warriors probably had to make do with a tough leather jerkin and a hardened leather cap. Scale armour, probably imported from Byzantium, is known from Sweden.

The Vikings' success depended not on superior equipment, organization or tactics—most Europeans waged war in a very similar way—but on their mobility, which kept them constantly one step ahead of the defenders. Their fast, shallow draughted ships were ideal for lightning attacks on coastal settlements or taking larger armies far inland along rivers. On land the Vikings campaigned as mounted infantry, covering long distances quickly on commandeered horses. By the time the local defences had been mustered, the Vikings would be long gone. In the 12th century, traditional infantry tactics were abandoned in favour of armoured cavalry.

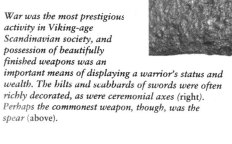

War was the most prestigious activity in Viking-age Scandinavian society, and possession of beautifully finished weapons was an important means of displaying a warrior's status and wealth. The hilts and scabbards of swords were often richly decorated, as were ceremonial axes (right). Perhaps the commonest weapon, though, was the spear (above).

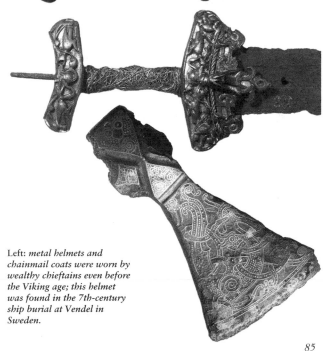

Left: *metal helmets and chainmail coats were worn by wealthy chieftains even before the Viking age; this helmet was found in the 7th-century ship burial at Vendel in Sweden.*

85

IV: The North Atlantic Saga

The Viking expansion in the North Atlantic was very different from the Viking raids in the British Isles—from the start, settlement was the main motive. Though Danes and Swedes were involved, the settlement of the Faeroe Islands, Iceland and Greenland was dominated by emigrants from Norway.

Above: The Vesturhorn on Iceland's rugged southeast coast would have been many settlers' first sight of their new homeland.

The first explorers of the North Atlantic were Irish monks, whose practice of *peregrinatio*—sailing into voluntary exile for God—had given them an unrivalled knowledge of the northern seas. These voyages were acts of faith, and the monks trusted to God to bring them to a safe landfall. No doubt a great many of them must have vanished without trace, but by around 700 Irish monks were living on the Faeroe Islands as hermits and by 800 they had discovered Iceland, which they called Thule, and even sailed beyond it to the frozen sea.

The Viking expansion in this area was originally a by-product of the raids on the Scottish islands which began at the end of the 8th century. The environment of the isles is similar to that of western Norway, and in the first half of the 9th century Norwegians began to settle permanently in the area. Here they will have come into contact with Irish monks, and it was probably from them that the Vikings learned of the existence of land to the north.

Beyond the Control of Kings

In Icelandic tradition, the settlement of the Faeroes and Iceland is held to have been begun by exiles fleeing the tyrannical rule that king Harald Finehair is said to have imposed after his victory at Hafrsfjord. This is unlikely to be the whole story. The battle of Hafrsfjord is believed to have taken place between 885 and 900 but, according to the Irish monk Dicuil, Vikings had reached the Faeroes and frightened off the Irish hermits there by the time he was writing in 825. The settlement of Iceland had also begun before Hafrsfjord. The first Vikings to reach Iceland were off-course seafarers *c.* 860 and the first settlers began to arrive about 10 years later, at which time Harald Finehair is unlikely to have been much more than a toddler. Iceland was not fully settled until *c.* 930, so Harald's rule may have played a part in sustaining emigration, but it cannot have been the initial cause.

However, there may be a wider truth in the Icelandic tradition. The leaders of the settlements were aristocrats of middling rank—local chieftains— there were no jarls or kings among them. The local chieftains were the main losers by the growth of centralized authority in Scandinavia in the 8th and 9th centuries, and the opportunity to emigrate to a new land beyond the control of kings must have been attractive to them. The government of Iceland, with its system of district *things* and the national *Althing* in which the chieftains or *goðar* played the leading role, was probably very similar to traditional forms of government before the rise of royal power in Scandinavia. The only significant national official was the Lawspeaker, an elective position with no executive authority. Decision making was a consensual process and though only the *goðar* could vote in the *Althing*, the need- ed to consider the wishes of their supporters as freemen could withdraw their allegiance if they wished. The peaceful adoption of Christianity as the official religion in Iceland by a vote of the *Althing* in 1000 was probably the greatest achievement of this form of government.

While the *goðar* were all of roughly similar wealth and status, the Icelandic system worked well. However, the *goðar* were not a closed class, and though the status could be inherited, men could fall out of the class or rise into it. In time a few pre-eminent chiefly families emerged, the consensual system broke down and in the 13th century civil wars broke out as they fought each other for supremacy. In desperation the Icelanders turned to Hakon IV, King of Norway, to restore order and in 1263 the country was formally annexed to Norway. In the end, the Icelandic colony succumbed to the forces of centralization from which its founders had believed they were escaping.

A significant number of the original settlers of Iceland came from the Norse colonies in the Hebrides. Several of the leading settlers were second-genera- tion emigrants, the product of mixed Norse-Celtic marriages, and some were already Christians. The settlement of Iceland coincided with a period of strengthening Celtic resistance to the Vikings, and it is likely that this prompted this exodus of otherwise apparently well established Norse set- tlers—there was no hostile native population in Iceland to threaten the long-term survival of the settlements.

Exodus to Greenland

The settlement of Greenland was probably a result of population pressure in Iceland. Greenland was discovered accidently by a storm-driven seafarer around 930, but its hostile, ice-bound appearance excited little interest until Erik the Red, a man with many enemies, rounded Cape Farewell some time around 983, looking for a safe place to spend his exile from Iceland, and discovered the ice-free eastern fjords. By this time, all the good land in Iceland had long been settled. Many latecomers, like Erik himself, were living on marginal land, so there was no shortage of potential settlers willing to emigrate to Greenland.

Though fascinating in its own right, the Norse discovery of America *c. 1000* cannot be said to have great historical significance. True, it is a tribute to the seafaring skills and adventurous spirit of the Vikings, but it was in reality the last gasp of their westward expansion. The distances were too great, the Vikings' numbers too few, their ships too fragile and the natives too hostile for the brief Norse attempt at settlement to have been sustainable. The discovery was soon forgotten outside Iceland, and it made no contribution to the later European exploration and colonization of the Americas which began at the end of the 15th century.

The Faeroes, Iceland and Greenland are bleak and inhospitable places to settle but they would not have appeared unattractive to a 9th-century Norwegian. What the settlers were looking for primarily was good grazing land—arable farming was not important in Norway —and grass grows well

Right: Traditional haymaking in the Faeroe Islands. Though bleak and treeless, the Faeroes had good pastureland for sheep and cattle, making them attractive to Norwegian settlers.

in the Faeroes and Iceland. The climate was milder in the early Middle Ages than it is today, and it was possible even in Greenland to grow a little grain. The Faeroes and Greenland were treeless, but Iceland had abundant birch woodland at the time of the settlement, though this was unsuitable for shipbuilding. The colonies' lack of timber for shipbuilding was a serious disadvantage. Once the ships used by the original settlers had decayed, they could be replaced only with great difficulty, and the colonies' vital trade links passed increasingly under foreign control. Both Iceland and Greenland suffered severely from the climatic deterioration known as the "Little Ice Age" that began around 1200. In Iceland the problem was compounded by serious volcanic eruptions: the worst, from Mount Hekla in 1104, scattered ash over half the island and forced the abandonment of many farms. Some eruptions caused glaciers to melt, sending disastrous floods rushing into the lowlands with heavy loss of life. Iceland's population, which was about 60,000 at the end of the Viking period, had fallen by half by the 17th century. The Greenland colony, which had never numbered more than about 4000, was hit so severely that it had become extinct by 1500. The Greenlanders were not helped by their extreme cultural conservatism, which prevented them learning anything from contacts with the

Eskimos: to the very end they struggled to continue the farming economy of their Norwegian ancestors in the shadow of the advancing glaciers.

The settlements in the Faeroes and Iceland were the only permanent extensions to the Scandinavian world to result from the Viking expansion, and in this lies their main historical significance. Elsewhere in Europe, the Scandinavian settlers were absorbed by the native population within a few generations, leaving little behind to tell of their presence beyond place-names and loan words in the local language. In the Faeroes and Iceland, however, there was no native population, and the settlers retained an identity rooted in the west coast districts of Norway, from whose dialects the Faeroes and Iceland languages have developed. The Icelanders showed the emigrant's preoccupation with origins in their magnificent saga tradition. Alone of all the Germanic peoples, they preserved the pagan mythology and traditions of their ancestors, and eventually recorded it after their conversion to Christianity.

Right: *Bratthlid, Eirik the Red's farm in the Norse Greenland colony's Eastern Settlement. By the late 10th century the best land in Iceland was taken and the good grazing of the ice-free west coast of Greenland attracted many settlers.*

The Faeroes and Iceland

Viking settlement of the remote, mountainous Faeroe Islands led to the accidental discovery of Iceland.

The Faeroes are a mountainous and windswept chain of islands about 190 miles northwest of Shetland. According to the Faereyinga Saga, the first Viking settler was Grímur Kamban. His second name is of Irish origin, so he had probably spent some time in Ireland or the Hebrides. Most of the settlers, however, came directly from the Norwegian west-coast districts of Sogn, Rogaland and Agder. Settlement must have begun around 825, when the Irish monk Dicuil complained that the Vikings had scared away his brethren who had been using the islands as a retreat for over a century.

The climate is unsuitable for crop growing, but the islands have good grazing and sheep and cattle rearing became the basis of the economy. To take advantage of mountain pastures, islanders moved their animals up to aergi (shielings) for the summer months. The early history of the Faeroese settlements is obscure, but the land seems to have been claimed by a few aristocratic families who then divided it among their followers. By 895 the settlements had been brought under the direct control of the kings of Norway.

The Vikings had probably heard of Iceland from the Irish—later settlers were to find croziers, books and other evidence of monastic settlement— but the first Norse visitors arrived by accident. The first Viking to reach the island was probably Gardar the Swede, who was blown off course on a voyage to the Hebrides around 860. He made landfall near the Eastern Horn and spent a year circumnavigating Iceland, wintering on the north coast at Husavik. The land looked very promising and Gardar decided to name it after himself, Gardarsholm. Another accidental early visitor was Naddod, who landed on Iceland's east coast after being blown off course while sailing from Norway to the Faeroes.

1/The settlement of the Faeroes, c. 825–1100

★ ? pre-Viking cultivation
▫ ? pre-Viking cross slab
◎ Viking settlement
▲ Viking cemetery
⊞ site of *Thing* (island parliament)
† bishopric, c.1100
● Viking-age shieling

◇ *c. 825*
traditional site of first settlement by Grímur Kamban

Kunoy
Vidoy Fugloy
Kalsoy
Eiði
Tjørnuvik Funningur
Borðoy
Svinoy
Klaksvik
E y s t u r o y
S t r e y m o y
Vágar
Mykines ?
Kvivik
Torshavn
Tinganes ⊞ Nólsoy
†
Kirkjubøur
Sandoy
Sandur
Skúvoy ▫?
N
Suduroy Hov
0   50 kms
0   30 miles

Below: according to local tradition, Grimur Kamban, the first Norse settler of the Faeroe Islands, chose this sheltered bay on Funningsfjordur as the site of his farm. The patchwork of tiny hayfields surrounding the modern village dates from late Viking times.

Right: the forbidding southeast coast of Iceland was the first landfall for many of the earliest Norse explorers of Iceland. There were few safe harbours here and grazing was poor, so this part of Iceland never became densely populated. Most settlers followed the coast westwards to the more favourable western fjords.

2/The exploration of Iceland, c. 860–70

Gardar the Swede, c. 860

Naddod the Viking

Floki Vilgerdarson

PAPOS ▲ place name associated with Irish monks

🜖 active volcano

Shortly afterwards, Floki Vilgerdarson set out from Rogaland to explore the island. The expedition was not a great success. Floki spent the first winter on Breidafjord, but because he had neglected to gather winter fodder all his livestock starved to death. The sea-ice was slow breaking up that spring, and the bad weather forced him to spend the next winter on Borgarfjord. Thoroughly disillusioned by his experiences, Floki decided to call the new land Iceland. Though the name stuck, other members of his party gave more favourable reports, and by 870 settlers began to arrive.

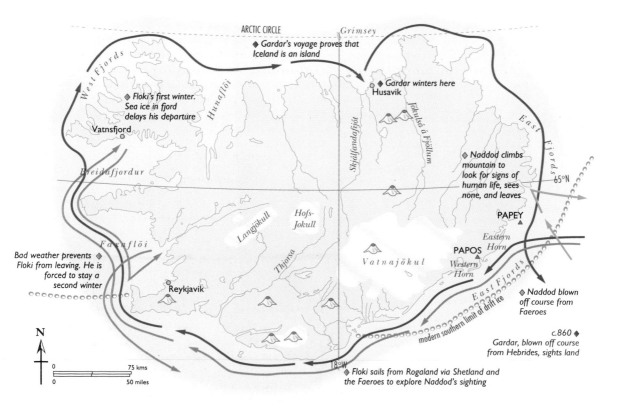

ARCTIC CIRCLE   *Grimsey*

◆ Gardar's voyage proves that Iceland is an island

West Fjords

◆ Floki's first winter. Sea ice in fjord delays his departure

Vatnsfjord

◆ Gardar winters here
Husavik

Hunaflói

Jökulsá á Fjöllum

Skjálfandafljót

◆ Naddod climbs mountain to look for signs of human life, sees none, and leaves

East Fjords

65°N

Breidafjordur

Langjökull

Hofs-Jokull

PAPEY ▲

Eastern Horn

Bad weather prevents Floki from leaving. He is forced to stay a second winter

Faxaflói

Thjorsa

Vatnajökul

PAPOS ▲
Western Horn

Reykjavik

◆ Naddod blown off course from Faeroes

East Fjords

modern southern limit of drift ice

c.860 ◆
Gardar, blown off course from Hebrides, sights land

N

0   75 kms
0   50 miles

18°W
◆ Floki sails from Rogaland via Shetland and the Faeroes to explore Naddod's sighting

The Settlement of Iceland

Vikings chiefs settle in Iceland, dividing the good grazing land round the coasts among their followers.

"A Norwegian named Ingolf... was the first to leave there for Iceland... He settled south in Reykjavik... At the time Iceland was covered with forest between mountain and seashore."
The Book of Icelanders, 12th century

The first settlers of Iceland were two foster-brothers, Ingolf and Hjorleif. They made a reconnoitre of the East Fjords in the late 860s, and around 870 returned to settle. Hjorleif was killed by his Irish slaves during the first winter, but after three years exploring Ingolf made a permanent settlement at Reykjavik. More settlers soon followed; most were from western Norway, but there were also Danes, Swedes and Scandinavians from the Hebrides. By 930 nearly all the good grazing land had been claimed. Except in the south-west, most of the settlements were close to the coast: the barren mountains and lava plains of the interior were, as they still remain, uninhabited.

The 12th-century Icelandic *Landnámabók* (The Book of the Settlements) identifies some 430 leaders of the settlement period. Mostly men of aristo-cratic background, they brought their families, personal retinues and slaves. They took personal possession of the land, farming some themselves and settling their retinues as tenants on the rest of their claim. Early settlements were lawless, and disputes often degenerated into protracted blood-feuds.

Local leadership was assumed by the *goðar*, wealthy chieftain-priests who were well placed to resolve or manipulate disputes and offer advocacy and protection to smaller landowners. They presided over the district assem-blies, or *Things*, which dealt with local disputes. In 930 an annual all-Iceland assembly, the *Althing*, was set up to deal with major disputes and establish common laws. Iceland was divided into four quarters which had equal vot-ing rights in the *Althing*. Only chieftains could vote, and the *Althing* remained an oligarchy, entirely under their control. In 1000, the *Althing* agreed to accept Christianity as the official religion, and the first bishopric was established at Skalholt in 1056. The system provided stable government until the 13th century, when the concentration of power in the hands of a few chiefly families led to civil war. As a result, Iceland came under direct rule from Norway in 1263.

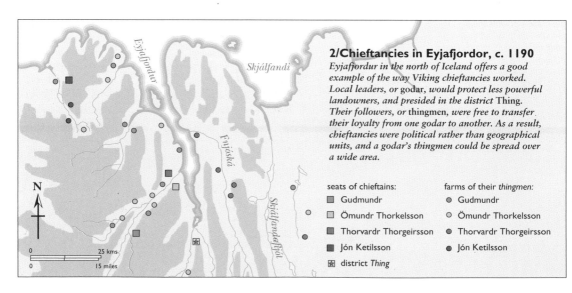

2/Chieftancies in Eyjafjordor, c. 1190
Eyjafjordur in the north of Iceland offers a good example of the way Viking chieftancies worked. Local leaders, or godar, would protect less powerful landowners, and presided in the district Thing. Their followers, or thingmen, were free to transfer their loyalty from one godar to another. As a result, chieftancies were political rather than geographical units, and a godar's thingmen could be spread over a wide area.

seats of chieftains:
- ■ Gudmundr
- □ Ömundr Thorkelsson
- ■ Thorvardr Thorgeirsson
- ■ Jón Ketilsson
- ✳ district *Thing*

farms of their *thingmen*:
- ● Gudmundr
- ○ Ömundr Thorkelsson
- ● Thorvardr Thorgeirsson
- ● Jón Ketilsson

0   25 kms
0   15 miles

N

Eyjafjordur
Skjálfandi
Frjóská
Skjálfandafljót

after J.L. Byock, Medieval Iceland

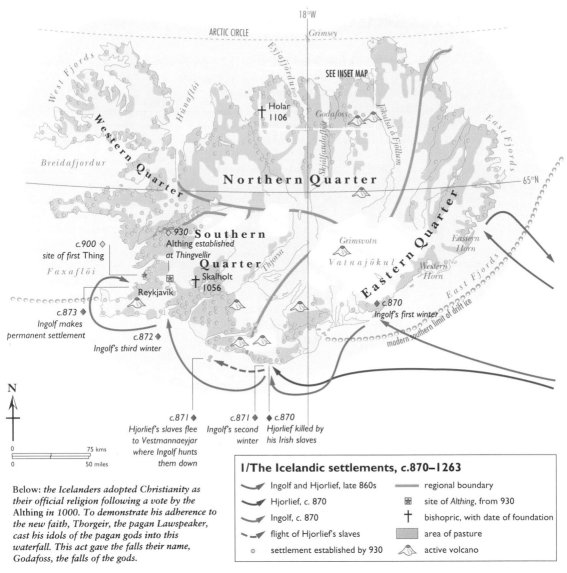

18°W

ARCTIC CIRCLE   *Grimsey*

West Fjords

Esjafjörðar

SEE INSET MAP

Húnaflói

Holar
1106

Godafoss

Jökulsá á Fjöllum

Western Quarter

Breiðafjörður

Northern Quarter

Skjálfandafljót

East Fjords

65°N

◊ *930* **Southern**
*Althing established
at Thingvellir*   **Quarter**

Skalholt
1056

Grimsvotn

Vatnajökul

Eastern Quarter

Eastern Horn

c.900 ◊
site of first Thing

Faxaflöi

Thjorsa

Western Horn

East Fjords

Reykjavik

◆ *c.870*
Ingolf's first winter

c.873 ◆
*Ingolf makes
permanent settlement*

modern southern limit of drift ice

c.872 ◆
Ingolf's third winter

N

0   75 kms
0   50 miles

c.871 ◆
*Hjorlief's slaves flee
to Vestmannaeyjar
where Ingolf hunts
them down*

c.871 ◆
*Ingolf's second
winter*

◆ *c.870*
*Hjorlief killed by
his Irish slaves*

Below: *the Icelanders adopted Christianity as
their official religion following a vote by the
Althing in 1000. To demonstrate his adherence to
the new faith, Thorgeir, the pagan Lawspeaker,
cast his idols of the pagan gods into this
waterfall. This act gave the falls their name,
Godafoss, the falls of the gods.*

1/The Icelandic settlements, *c.870–1263*

Ingolf and Hjorlief, late 860s	regional boundary
Hjorlief, *c.* 870	site of *Althing*, from 930
Ingolf, *c.* 870	bishopric, with date of foundation
flight of Hjorlief's slaves	area of pasture
settlement established by 930	active volcano

Icelandic Literature

Medieval Iceland occupies a special place in the history of European civilization as the home of one of Europe's oldest traditions of vernacular literature.

Iceland's isolation from Europe allowed its ancient Germanic myths, legends and storytelling traditions to survive, and its aristocratic social structure fostered a fascination with family history and national origins. Most old Icelandic literature was written down in the 12th and 13th centuries, but it includes much orally-transmitted material that was originally composed up to 200–300 years earlier. Shortly after Iceland lost its independence to Norway in 1263, its literary tradition began to decline, and by the later Middle Ages it had died out. Such is the conservatism of the Icelandic language, however, that modern Icelanders have less difficulty reading Old Icelandic literature than modern English speakers have in reading Shakespeare.

Old Icelandic literature consists of poetry and the prose works known as sagas. The poetry falls into two genres, Skaldic verse and Eddic verse. Skaldic verse is an important historical source, as these heroic poems were composed by court poets (*skalds*) to commemorate the achievements of their aristocratic and royal patrons. As such, they are hardly impartial accounts, but are often the most contemporary sources available for some 10th- and 11th-century events. The Eddic verses consist of a mixture of mythological and heroic poems, composed during the Viking age but containing material which may be several centuries older. The mythological poems, which describe the adventures of the Norse gods, are the most important—without them, we would know almost nothing about early

"Cattle die and kinsmen die,
And so dies one's self;
One thing I know that never dies,
The fame of a man's deeds."
The *Hávamál*

Right: *Egil Skallagrimsson, from a 17th-century manuscript of Egil's Saga. Brave warrior, murderer, merchant, farmer and great poet, Egil embodies the contradictory faces of the Viking age in a single, larger-than-life character. Many Viking-age poems attributed to him are incorporated into the saga.*

Right: *this late Icelandic manuscript shows scenes from pagan Norse mythology. On the left is the wolf Fenrir, a mortal enemy of the gods. They restrained Fenrir with chains, but at Ragnarök, the end of the world, he will break his bonds and devour Odin. On the right is Yggdrasil, the sacred ash tree which supports the universe.*

Far right: *a page from Harald Finehair's saga, part of Snorri Sturluson's* Heimskringla *(The Circle of the World). Snorri wrote this monumental history of the kings of Norway, which played an important part in forming the Norwegian national identity, around 1225. Though it contains much legendary material, it is one of the major historical sources for Viking-age Scandinavia. This early 14th-century manuscript, known as the Codex Frisiana after one of its owners, Otto Friis, is one of the finest of all medieval Icelandic books.*

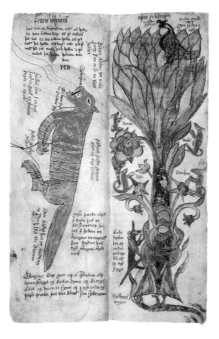

Above: *because its economy was dependent on cattle, medieval Iceland had plentiful supplies of calfskin—the raw material for vellum, the main writing material of the Middle Ages. As a result, books were relatively inexpensive and widely available. Most manuscripts were unilluminated and given cheap utilitarian bindings, like the sturdy wooden covers of this 14th-century copy of Njal's Saga.*

Germanic paganism. Medieval Icelanders were not ashamed of their pagan past and, alone among the Germanic peoples, they recorded their pagan myths and beliefs. The longest of the mythological poems, the *Hávamál*, (Sayings of the High One) is a body of ethical teachings attributed to Odin. Most of the sayings concern the everyday concerns of the peasant farmer, but in others the Viking love of fame and glory shines through.

The heroic poems in the Edda are largely concerned with legendary characters such as Sigurd the Volsung (Siegfried of the Niebelungenlied). Some real figures from the Migration Period, including Attila the Hun and the great Gothic King Ermaneric, also put in an appearance, but they have been transformed into the stuff of legends and their Eddic exploits bear no relation to historical reality.

The prose sagas include a wide range of genres from weighty narrative histories such as Snorri Sturluson's *Heimskringla*, an epic history of the kings of Norway, to myths, romances and supernatural tales. However, the most original works are the family sagas, historical novels based loosely on the personalities and events of Iceland's settlement period but mainly written in the 13th century. This was a time of social and political disintegration, and family sagas probably catered for an escapist desire to recreate a "golden age" of the past. A favourite theme of these sagas is the working out of a blood feud. In Njal's Saga, for example, bonds of kinship, personal loyalty and friendship inexorably draw Njal, a man of peace and goodwill, into quarrels not of his making, with ultimately fatal consequences. The authors of the family sagas were much concerned with the workings of fate. This does not mean that their characters are the pawns of blind fate, however; they control their destinies, and meet their fates as a consequence of their own weaknesses and errors. Compared to the chivalric romances then fashionable in western Europe, the family sagas are strikingly modern-seeming works written in a compellingly terse style and featuring psychologically realistic characters. The best of them—Njal's Saga, Egil's Saga and Laxdæla Saga—rank among the great works of European literature.

The Vikings in Greenland

At the edge of the known world, Norse settlers eked out a precarious existence along the sheltered fjords of western Greenland.

Above: an Eskimo carving of a Norse Greenlander. The settlers were culturally very conservative and made no effort to learn from the Eskimos' long experience of living in Arctic conditions. This probably contributed to the settlements' decline when the climate deteriorated after 1300.

Ice-bound Greenland owes its optimistic name to Erik the Red, who hoped it would attract settlers. The first Norsemen to sight Greenland were Gunnbjorn Ulf-Krakuson and Snaebjorn Galti, around 900 and 978 respectively. All they saw was the barren, glaciated east coast. But around 983, Erik discovered an ice-free region to the west, with sheltered fjords and good grazing. He returned to Iceland to persuade others to follow him, and in 986 set out again with 25 ships. Only 14 made it round Cape Farewell, but this was enough to found two settlements: the Eastern and, 300 miles further north, the Western.

At first the settlements flourished. The climate was milder than today and it was even possible to grow cereals in sheltered places. Cattle and sheep rearing was the basis of the economy, but the settlements' most valuable exports—walrus ivory and hide and polar bear furs—came from rich hunting grounds to the north. Even further north, the Norse traded with the Eskimos. At its peak, the Norse population numbered around 4000. The Eastern Settlement eventually included 190 farms, 12 parish churches, a cathedral, an Augustinian monastery and a Benedictine nunnery. The smaller Western Settlement had 90 farms and four churches. Between the two was the Middle Settlement of 20 farms. The settlers were probably organized on Icelandic lines, with Erik the Red taking a role akin to the Law-speaker.

The Greenlanders lost their independence in 1261 when they came under Norwegian rule. Soon after 1300 the climate began to deteriorate. Stock-rearing suffered and sea-ice cut the settlers off from the outside world for years at a time. The Eskimos began to move south and there were violent clashes with the Greenlanders. By 1410, the date of the last recorded contact, only the Eastern Settlement survived. Archaeological excavations have shown that some contacts continued after this date, but a ship reaching the Eastern Settlement in 1540 found only deserted farms and, in one of them, a single unburied body.

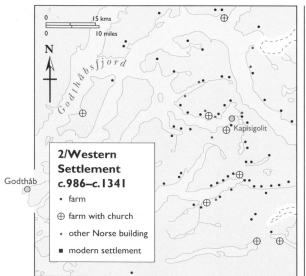

2/Western Settlement c.986–c.1341
- • farm
- ⊕ farm with church
- • other Norse building
- ■ modern settlement

Godthåbsfjord

Godthåb

Kapisigolit

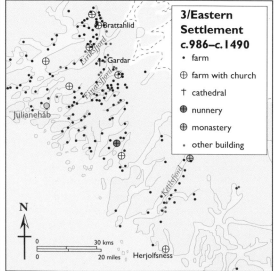

3/Eastern Settlement c.986–c.1490
- • farm
- ⊕ farm with church
- † cathedral
- ⊕ nunnery
- ⊕ monastery
- • other building

Brattahlid

Gardar

Einarsfjord

Julianehåb

Eiriksfjord

Ketilsfjord

Herjolfsness

90°

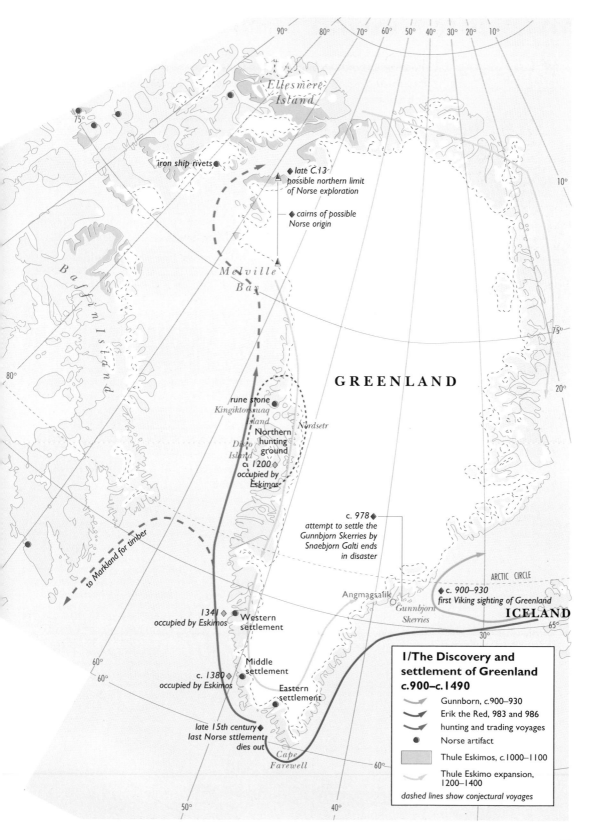

Ellesmere Island

75°

iron ship rivets •

◆ late C.13
possible northern limit
of Norse exploration

◆ cairns of possible
Norse origin

Baffin Island

Melville Bay

80°

GREENLAND

rune stone •
Kingiktorsuaq
Island

Nordsetr

Northern
hunting
ground

Disco
Island

c. 1200 ◆
occupied by
Eskimos

c. 978 ◆
attempt to settle the
Gunnbjorn Skerries by
Snaebjorn Galti ends
in disaster

to Markland for timber

ARCTIC CIRCLE

Angmagsalik

Gunnbjorn
Skerries

◆ c. 900–930
first Viking sighting of Greenland

ICELAND

1341 ◆
occupied by Eskimos

Western
settlement

60°

Middle
settlement

c. 1380 ◆
occupied by Eskimos

Eastern
settlement

late 15th century ◆
last Norse sttlement
dies out

Cape
Farewell

60°

50°

40°

**I/The Discovery and
settlement of Greenland
c.900–c.1490**

Gunnborn, c.900–930

Erik the Red, 983 and 986

hunting and trading voyages

• Norse artifact

Thule Eskimos, c.1000–1100

Thule Eskimo expansion,
1200–1400

dashed lines show conjectural voyages

Voyages to Vinland

Viking expansion reached its westernmost limits as seafarers from Greenland established a foothold on the North American continent.

Above: a spindle whorl found at L'Anse aux Meadows. Since spinning was a female occupation in Viking societies, such finds show that there were women among the settlers.

The Icelandic sagas tell how, around 985, Bjarni Herjolfsson was blown off course from Greenland, and made a chance sighting of land to the west. Some 15 years later, Leif Eiriksson set out from the Eastern Settlement in Greenland to investigate Bjarni's sighting. Sailing to the northwest, he first came upon a land of bare rock and glaciers which he called Helluland (Slab Land). Sailing south he next reached a low, forested land. This he called Markland (Wood Land), Leif pressed on still further south and spent a winter in a land with a mild climate, where grapes grew wild and rivers teemed with salmon. Leif called this Vinland (Wine Land).

The locations of his discoveries will probably never be established with absolute certainty. Helluland was probably Baffin Island; Markland was almost certainly Labrador. Identifying Vinland is more difficult. The only Norse settlement so far discovered in North America is at l'Anse aux Meadows in Newfoundland, but this is too far north to fit the saga descriptions. Vinland probably lay south of the Gulf of St Lawrence, the approximate northern limit of the wild grapes, but north of Cape Cod, the southern limit of the Atlantic salmon.

Leif's voyage was followed up by attempts to settle permanently in Vinland, occasionally voyages from treeless Greenland to collect timber from Markland continued as late as 1347. The only Norse artifact so far found south of Newfoundland is a coin of King Olaf the Peaceful of Norway (1066–93) from an Indian site at Godard Point in Maine. This is not enough to prove that the Norse were ever there: the Indians may have obtained it by trading with the Inuit of the Canadian Arctic, who were in direct contact with the Norse settlements in Greenland.

"Leif set sail when he was ready; he ran into prolonged difficulties at sea, and finally came upon lands whose existence he had never suspected. There were fields of wild wheat growing there, and vines, and among the trees were maples."
Eirik's Saga

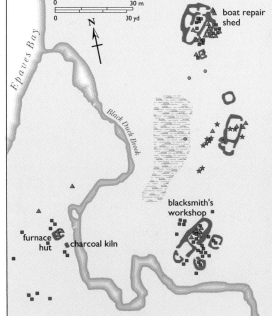

2/The Viking settlement at L'Anse aux Meadows
This cluster of turf houses could have accommodated about 90 people, It was occupied for no more than a few years—from around 1000–1020, according to radiocarbon dates. This settlement may have served as a base for voyages to the south; butternuts (which do not grow north of the St Lawrence River) have been found on the site. Some fishing and hunting went on, but there is no evidence of farming. The main activity was carpentry and blacksmithing associated with ship repair.

▲ foundations
▲ iron rivets
■ iron slag
★ other Norse artefact
● butternuts

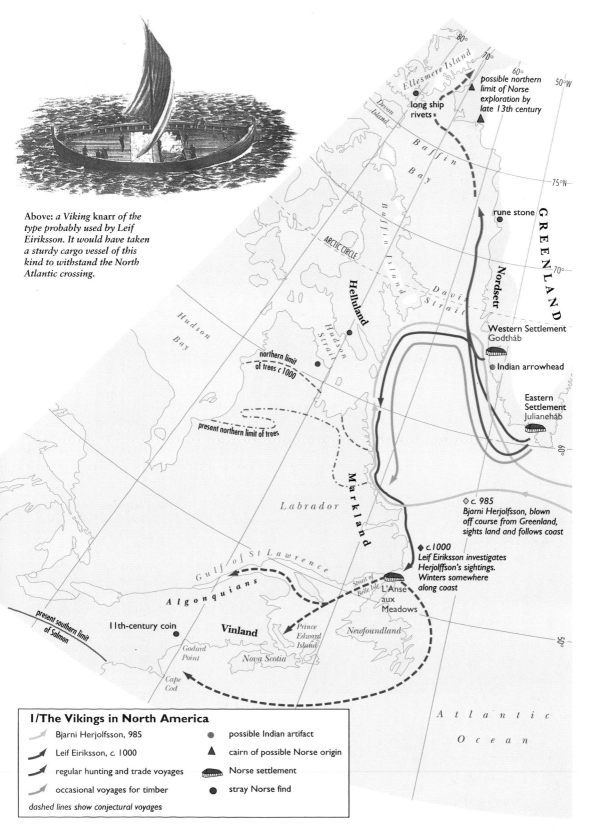

Above: *a Viking* knarr *of the type probably used by Leif Eiriksson. It would have taken a sturdy cargo vessel of this kind to withstand the North Atlantic crossing.*

80°

70°

60°

50°W

possible northern limit of Norse exploration by late 13th century

long ship rivets

Ellesmere Island

Devon Island

Baffin Bay

75°N

rune stone

GREENLAND

ARCTIC CIRCLE

Baffin Island

Davis Strait

Nordsetr

70°

Helluland

Hudson Strait

Hudson Bay

Western Settlement
Godthâb

Indian arrowhead

northern limit of trees c 1000

Eastern Settlement
Julianehâb

60°

present northern limit of trees

Labrador

◇ c. 985
Bjarni Herjolfsson, blown off course from Greenland, sights land and follows coast

Markland

◆ c.1000
Leif Eiriksson investigates Herjolffson's sightings. Winters somewhere along coast

Gulf of St Lawrence

Strait of Belle Isle

L'Anse aux Meadows

Algonquians

50°

present southern limit of Salmon

11th-century coin

Vinland

Prince Edward Island

Newfoundland

Godard Point

Nova Scotia

Cape Cod

Atlantic Ocean

1/The Vikings in North America

Bjarni Herjolfsson, 985	● possible Indian artifact
Leif Eiriksson, c. 1000	▲ cairn of possible Norse origin
regular hunting and trade voyages	Norse settlement
occasional voyages for timber	● stray Norse find

dashed lines show conjectural voyages

V: The Vikings in the East

Swedish traders sailed far up Russia's rivers to dominate the lucrative routes to the East. Their ranks were swelled by Viking mercenaries on their way to join the Byzantine emperor's elite Varangian guard. These Scandinavians, known to their contemporaries as the Rus, gave Russia its name and its first centralized state, before adopting the language and lifestyle of their Slavic subjects and the religion and culture of the Byzantines.

The Viking movement east was dominated by the Swedes. Two terms are used to describe the Swedish Vikings in the east: *Rús* and *Væringjar*, or Varangian. Rus is probably derived from *Ruotsi*, the Finnish name for the Swedes, which itself probably derives from the Scandinavian *rôðr*, meaning a crew of oarsmen. Rus is only ever used to describe Scandinavians living in Russia (which gets its name from the Rus), never from the homelands. Varangian is derived from Old Norse *várar*, pledge or oath, and means "men of the pledge". The name, which only dates from the mid-10th century, probably came into use to distinguish newly arrived Scandinavian mercenaries and traders from the increasingly Slavicized Rus.

Below: Many rune stones from Sweden record exploits in the east. This inscription from Uppland is a memorial to Ragnvald who had served as a mercenary in the Byzantine army.

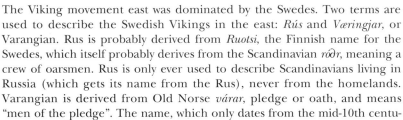

Scandinavian expansion east of the Baltic predates the outbreak of Viking raiding in the west by more than a century. From the beginning it was dominated by trade and the closely related activity of tribute-gathering. Scandinavian merchant graves from the east Baltic trading settlements at Elbing and Grobin show that the earliest phase of this expansion began around 650. A hundred years later Scandinavians were living at the Finnish market centre of Staraja Ladoga ("Aldeigjuborg" to the Vikings), an excellent base for the exploitation of the northern fur-trapping grounds. Up to this point, the Scandinavians were probably still thinking mainly in terms of supplying western markets. Staraja Ladoga also had a commanding position on the river routes that gave easy access to the heart of Russia. When, at the end of the 8th century, Arab merchants began to penetrate the Volga, they introduced fine quality silver coins into circulation in Russia, providing the Scandinavians with the motive to press inland to discover their source. By the 830s the Rus, as they were now known, had completed their exploration of the Russian river system and had established direct trade contacts with the Arab traders on the Volga and with the Byzantines at Constantinople. The Russian river system was an ideal highway for long distance trade. The rivers Lovat (flowing to Lake Ladoga and the Gulf of Finland), Dvina (to the Gulf of Riga and the Baltic), Dneipr (to the Black Sea) and Volga (to the Caspian) all have

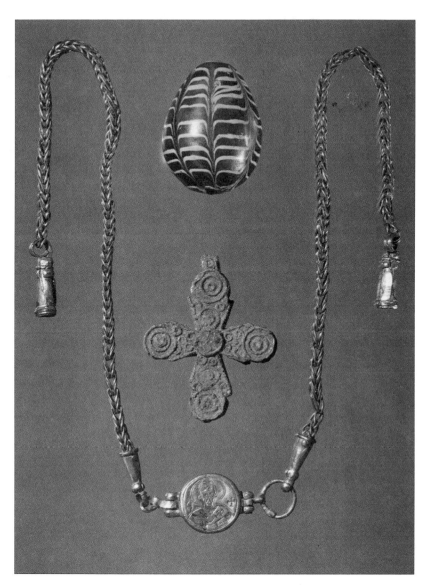

Right: *The Rus quickly adopted the Greek Orthodox religion of their Byzantine neighbours to the south, while maintaining trade links with their Scandinavian homelands. These Byzantine-style Christian artefacts found their way from Kiev to Scandinavia: glazed pottery Easter egg, a bronze cross, and a silver locket pendant made to hold a relic.*

navigable headwaters rising within a few miles of each other in the hill country south of Novgorod. Except for short distances where ships had to be portaged—carried or drawn overland—from the headwaters of one river system to another, or to avoid rapids, it was possible to sail the light, shallow draughted Viking ships all the way from the Baltic to the Caspian or the Black Sea.

Novgorod and Kiev

Though trade was the main driving force behind this movement, it was not entirely peaceful. The routes through Russia were dangerous, and traders ran a great risk of attack by the local Slavs or steppe nomads, especially at the impassable Dneipr rapids south of Kiev where boats had to be drawn overland. Viking raiders sometimes followed the routes the traders had pioneered to launch raids on Constantinople and the Islamic lands around the Caspian Sea, though without conspicuous success. It is also unlikely that the

Above: The lure of Arab silver was the driving force of Swedish expansion into eastern Europe. The thousands of Arab dirhems found in hoards, such as this one from the island of Gotland, represent only a fraction of the wealth that flooded into Scandinavia from the east during the Viking age.

Rus state based on Kiev and Novgorod, which developed in the second half of the 9th century, was established without subjugating the neighbouring Slavs first. According to the 12th-century Russian Primary Chronicle, the Varangian Rus first made the Slavic and Finnish tribes of Russia into tributaries, but were then driven out. However, disputes among the tribes persuaded them to invite the Rus to come back to rule over them and keep order. Around 862, three brothers arrived with their kinsfolk. The eldest, Rurik, established himself at Novgorod, the second at Beloozero and the third at Izborsk. When his brothers died, Rurik became ruler of the whole of northwest Russia.

Some time later, two Rus chieftains from Novgorod, Askold and Dir, sailed down the Dneipr and captured the hilltop town of Kiev. Novgorod and Kiev were rival Rus centres until Rurik's successor Oleg captured the town and made it his capital around 882. Though the story of the Slavs' invitation to the Varangians was no doubt invented to give the authority of the Kievan dynasty a legitimate basis, in general outline it is probably accurate. After a period of tribute gathering, independent Rus leaders took control of the trading settlements of northwest Russia, from which they subjugated the surrounding Slav population. Eventually the ruler of Novgorod (probably Rurik, though his existence is doubted by some historians) was recognized by all the Rus, but two leaders broke away and established a rival centre at Kiev which was later captured by Oleg, who made it his main residence.

The importance of the Scandinavian contribution to the development of the Kievan Rus state is the most controversial issue in the history of the Viking expansion in the east. Unfortunately the subject has been bedevilled by competing nationalisms and, in the Soviet period, by political ideology—there are some Russian historians who would maintain that the Rus were

Slavs. However, the original Scandinavian identity of the Rus is not in doubt, as the Annals of St Bertin, the earliest source to mention them, make clear in their account of an embassy which was sent to Louis the Pious from the Byzantine Emperor Theophilus in 839: "[Theophilus] also sent with the envoys some men who said they—meaning their whole people—were called 'Rhos' and had been sent to him by their king who was called Khagan for the sake of friendship, so they claimed. When the emperor [*i.e.* Louis] investigated the reason for their coming here, he discovered that they belonged to the people of the Swedes." (*The Annals of St. Bertin*, J.L. Nelson, Manchester University Press 1991). A slightly later Arab writer, Al-Ya'qubi, also identifies the Rus as being of the same race as the pirates who attacked Seville in 843–44. The names of the earliest rulers of the Rus state—Rurik, Oleg (Helgi) and Igor (Ingvar)—are also clearly of Scandinavian rather than Slavic origin.

There can be little doubt then that the first rulers of the Kievan Russian state were Scandinavians, and that it was their initiative that led to the creation of the state as a political entity. It was also largely due to the activities of Scandinavian merchants that Russia experienced rapid urban growth in the 10th century. For example, the Rus transformed Novgorod from a minor Slavic settlement on the island of Gorodisce into a major fortified market centre in the 9th century, before moving the whole settlement to a larger fortified site (the "New Fortress" from which the city gets its name) a few miles to the north in the 10th century. Because of the Scandinavian connection, early Kievan Rus also had wider ranging connections with the rest of Europe than any succeeding Russian state would enjoy before the 18th century.

Scandinavians and Slavs

It is doubtful, however, that Scandinavian influence played much part in shaping the cultural development of Kievan Rus. The Slavic peoples of eastern Europe were at a very similar level of social and technological development as the Vikings. They were skilful ironworkers and craftsmen, active traders and efficient farmers while many of their fortified settle-

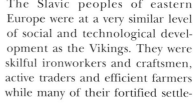

Right: The Rus travelled as far as the Black and Caspian seas, where they traded with Arab merchants of the Abbasid caliphate. Arab vessels of pottery, silver and bronze have been found at Viking settlements in Russia.

ments were fast approaching true urban status. They may have lacked the unity and purposeful leadership of the Rus, but they had very little to learn from them. Indeed, the limited nature of Scandinavian cultural influence on the development of early Russia is immediately obvious from the fact that there are only six or seven Scandinavian loan words in the Russian language. Neither is there any apparent Scandinavian influence on early Russian law, institutions or religion.

In fact the most important cultural influence on Kievan Russia was not Scandinavian but Byzantine. Prince Vladimir's conversion to Orthodox Christianity in 989 opened Russia to the powerful civilizing influence of the Byzantine Empire, and ensured that the country would develop a cultural identity which was quite distinct from the Latin-influenced west. Kievan Russia's alphabet, literature, architecture, music, art, law, education system and political ideologies were all fundamentally Byzantine in origin.

Though the Scandinavian presence in Russia is well attested archaeologically—for example, the 187 Viking oval brooches found there far exceeds the number found in western Europe—it is clear from the evidence of Viking-age cemeteries that the Rus were a minority among the Slavic population even in the towns—and there is no evidence at all of Scandinavian rural settlement. The Rus must have formed a warrior and merchant elite, but despite a stream of new arrivals from Scandinavia continuing into the 11th century, they became increasingly influenced by the Slavs, with whom they intermarried and allied. A sign of this is the adoption of Slavic names by the ruling dynasty. The first Rus ruler to have a Slavic name, Igor's son Svyatoslav, came to power in 945 and his son Vladimir (978–1015) worshipped the Slavic god Perun before his conversion to Christianity. By the mid-10th century, Slavs formed an important component of Rus armies, and even numbered among the commanders. There was still a distinction between the language of the Rus and that of the Slavs at this time, but Slavic speakers must have been the majority among the ruling classes because Slavic became the language of the church after the conversion to Christianity in 989. Certainly by the 11th century the Rus were, to all intents and purposes, Slavic in language and culture. In all the process of assimilation to the native population had taken about 150 years to complete: about the same length of time as it took for the Viking settlers in England to lose their Scandinavian identity.

Dynastic links with Scandinavia remained strong in the 11th century, and Viking warriors continued to pass through on their way to join the Varangian guard at Constantinople, but the merchants were mostly gone. The exhaustion of the Islamic world's silver mines between 965 and 1015 led to the decline and eventual abandonment of the trade routes to the east. After 1066 fewer warriors came, and the ranks of the Byzantine emperor's Varangian guard of "axe wielding barbarians" were increasingly filled with exiled Anglo-Saxons.

Vikings in the Baltic

Perhaps the area of Viking activity about which least is known is the Baltic, which in the 9th and 10th centuries must have been something of a Viking lake. The paucity of our knowledge is due to the lack of contemporary written sources for this period; the Slavs and Balts who lived on the south and east shores of the Baltic were illiterate, while the Vikings' own runic alphabet was only suitable for short inscriptions. Nor were western Europeans much interested in Slav-Scandinavian relations before the late 10th century.

The West Slavs or Wends had a large number of trading towns along the southern Baltic coast, and finds of large quantities of Arabic silver coins show that they were tied in in an important way with the Baltic and Russian trade routes. The Wends were warlike, and though the Danes and Swedes occasionally managed to take control of a trading town on the coast, such as the unidentified Reric in the early 9th century, they made no headway inland. Later saga accounts speak of great Vikings like Olaf Tryggvason cutting their teeth on raids in the Baltic against the Slavs and Balts, and there can be no doubt, even in the absence of more reliable sources, that they did suffer a great deal of Viking raiding. However, the most famous Vikings of the Baltic, the Jomsvikings are almost certainly legendary. The Jomsvikings are said to have been a sworn fellowship of elite Vikings who sold their services to the highest bidder. Somewhat improbably, judging from what more contemporary sources have to tell us about the Viking appetite for the opposite sex, women were forbidden to enter their fortress at Jomsborg— probably Wolin, at the mouth of the Oder. Excavations have shown that in the 10th century there was a fortified trading settlement and Slavic cult centre there, with a population that included Scandinavians as well as Slavs. It does not quite live up to the saga description of a great fortress with an artificial harbour for 360 ships, but perhaps a band of Scandinavian mercenaries serving a Slavic prince there might have given rise to the legend. There was a certain amount of cultural interchange between the West Slavs and the Scandinavians. The Scandinavians may have learned bridge-building techniques from the Slavs, while they learned shipbuilding from the Scandinavians. In this the Slavs had decidedly the better part of the bargain, and in the 11th century they applied their new found skills to give the Scandinavians a dose of their own medicine.

Below: These Viking runes were probably carved into the polished marble of the cathedral of Hagia Sophia in Constantinople by a member of the Byzantine emperor's elite Varangian guard. The inscription has not been fully deciphered but it includes the name Halfdan.

The Swedes in the East

Swedish adventurers travel along the rivers of Russia to found a trading empire stretching from the Baltic to the Black Sea.

"The Chuds, the Slavs, the Krivichians and the Ves then said to the people of the Rus, "Our land is great and rich, but there is no order in it. Come to rule and reign over us."
Russian Primary Chronicle, c. 1113

While the Viking expansion westward was dominated by Danes and Norwegians, that to the east was dominated by the Swedes. Known as the "Rus", from the Finnish word for Swede, they eventually gave their name to the Russian state. Their eastward expansion was motivated primarily by the desire to control trade routes. It began well before the start of what is normally regarded as the Viking Age: even before 700, Slav and Balt towns such as Elbing and Grobin had significant permanent Scandinavian populations, and by the mid-8th century, Scandinavians were living at the Finnish settlement at Staraja Ladoga on the River Lovat. By the early 9th century, the Rus were navigating the Volga and the Lovat-Dneiper river systems to make direct trading contacts with the Abbasid Caliphate and the Byzantine Empire far to the south.

During the course of the 9th century the Rus founded merchant towns such as Novgorod, or won control of existing Slav towns such Kiev and used them as bases from which to subjugate their hinterlands. By the 860s Novgorod had emerged as the predominant Rus centre under its semi-legendary ruler Rurik, who is commonly regarded as the founder of the Russian state. Around 882 Oleg, Rurik's kinsman and successor, took control of Kiev and made it the capital of a state that stretched from the Gulf of Finland almost to the Black Sea. Though the Rus gave their name to Russia, nowhere in the vast Kievan state were Scandinavians in a majority. Even the towns were predominantly Slavic in character, and there is no evidence of Scandinavian rural settlement. The Rus were a military and merchant elite who

Below: this manuscript illustration, from the work of the Byzantine historian John Scylitzes, shows a Russian attack on Constantinople being driven off by Byzantine cavalry.

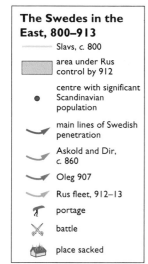

The Swedes in the East, 800–913

——— Slavs, c. 800

[shaded box] area under Rus control by 912

● centre with significant Scandinavian population

main lines of Swedish penetration

Askold and Dir, c. 860

Oleg 907

Rus fleet, 912–13

portage

battle

place sacked

exacted tribute in furs and slaves from their Slav subjects to trade with the Arabs for silver.

Once established at Kiev, the Rus were within easy striking distance of the Black Sea and its rich coasts. Like the Vikings in the west, the Rus were not inclined to trade if they thought they could take what they wanted by force, and in 860 and 907 savage but unsuccessful attacks were made on the Byzantine capital Constantinople. The second attack was followed by trade treaties in 907 and 911. Viking fleets also penetrated the Caspian Sea. The greatest of these raids was in 912–13, and followed an agreement by which the Rus agreed to share half the plunder from the expedition with the Khazar khan in return for permission to sail through Khazar territory. The Rus found the Muslim lands around the Caspian Sea virtually defenceless, but news of their atrocities so outraged the Khazars that they went back on their agreement and ambushed and destroyed the Rus fleet on its way home.

Above: *a Byzantine bronze coin depictiing the Emperor Leo VI, kown as "the Wise" (r. 886–912). Having driven off a Viking attack on Constantinople in 907, he recognized the fighting qualities of the Rus, and included provisions for recruiting them as mercenaries in the 911 treaty.*

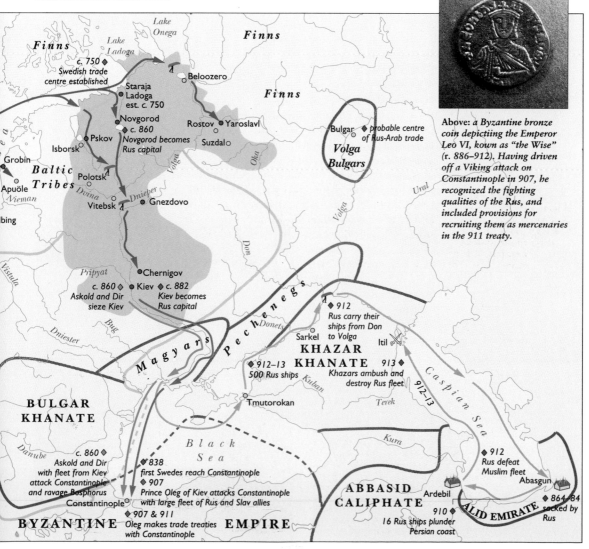

From Scandinavian to Slav

Like the Vikings in the west, the Rus were absorbed by the peoples they conquered, and in a few generations they adopted Slavic names and culture.

"I have never seen more perfect physical specimens, tall as date palms, blond and ruddy. They wear neither tunics nor kaftans, but each man wears a cape which covers one side of his body, leaving one hand free. Each man has an axe, a sword, and a knife, and keeps them by him at all times… They are the filthiest of God's creatures."

the Arab merchant Ibn Fadlan meets Rus traders at Itil, 922

The process of the assimilation first becomes apparent in the reign of Oleg's successor Igor (912–45). The Rus signatories to the trade treaty agreed between Oleg and the Byzantines in 911 had all had Scandinavian names; but when Igor agreed a similar treaty with Byzantium after his unsuccessful attack in 944, several of the Rus signatories had Slav names. Igor was the last Rus ruler to have a Scandinavian name (Igor is a variant of Ingvar); the name of his successor Svyatoslav (945–72) is Slavic. Many Scandinavians still fought in Svyatoslav's armies, however, and he himself was the epitome of a pagan Viking conqueror. He campaigned against the Khazars and the Volga and Danubian Bulgars, adding huge areas to the Kievan state, but these were all lost after his death. By the reign of Vladimir I (978–1015), Slavonic influence came to dominate the Kievan state. With the adoption of Orthodox Christianity as the state religion in 988, Byzantium became the main external influence on Russian development. By the time Kievan Rus reached the zenith of its power in the reign of Yaroslav the Wise (1019–54), the Rus were thoroughly Slavic in character.

Around 965 the flow of Arab silver through Russia to Scandinavia began to dry up as the Muslim world's silver mines became exhausted. The Scandinavians sought new sources of silver, and a new wave of Viking raids erupted in the west. This time, Swedes took part, and by 1015 they had abandoned their eastern trade routes. But the memory of the wealth of the east persisted for another generation, and around 1041 Ingvar the Widefarer, a Swede, made a famous attempt to re-open the trade routes with the Arab east. A remarkable group of runestones in central Sweden commemorate many of the men who died with Ingvar when his expedition met with disaster in "Serkland", probably somewhere in central Asia.

Right: the Golden Gate at Kiev was built during the reign of Yaroslav the Wise (1019–54). Although defensive in form, its grandeur suggests that its main purpose was to advertise the wealth and power of Kievan Rus. (The church on the second storey was added at a later date.)

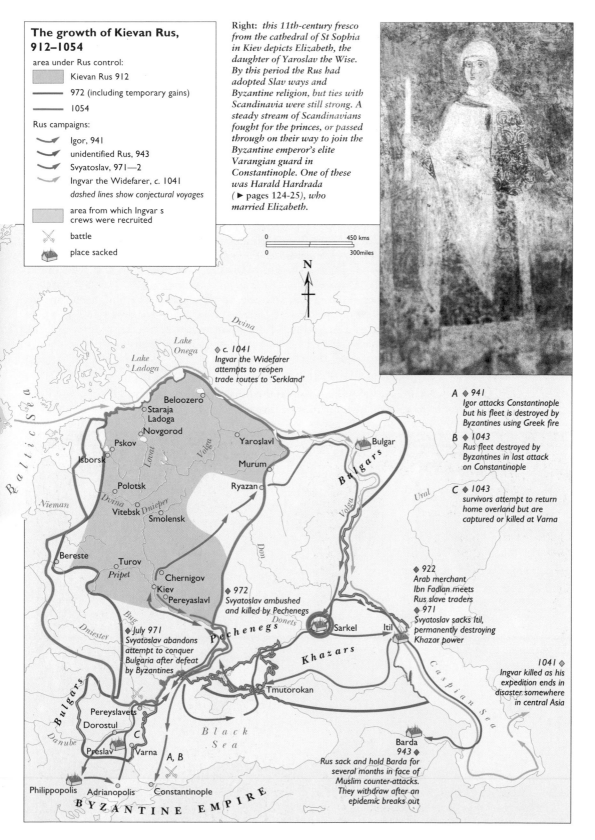

The growth of Kievan Rus, 912–1054

area under Rus control:

Kievan Rus 912

—————— 972 (including temporary gains)

————— 1054

Rus campaigns:

Igor, 941

unidentified Rus, 943

Svyatoslav, 971—2

Ingvar the Widefarer, c. 1041

dashed lines show conjectural voyages

area from which Ingvar s crews were recruited

⚔ battle

🏰 place sacked

0 450 kms

0 300 miles

N

Right: this 11th-century fresco from the cathedral of St Sophia in Kiev depicts Elizabeth, the daughter of Yaroslav the Wise. By this period the Rus had adopted Slav ways and Byzantine religion, but ties with Scandinavia were still strong. A steady stream of Scandinavians fought for the princes, or passed through on their way to join the Byzantine emperor's elite Varangian guard in Constantinople. One of these was Harald Hardrada (▶ pages 124-25), who married Elizabeth.

◆ c. 1041
Ingvar the Widefarer attempts to reopen trade routes to 'Serkland'

A ◆ 941
Igor attacks Constantinople but his fleet is destroyed by Byzantines using Greek fire

B ◆ 1043
Rus fleet destroyed by Byzantines in last attack on Constantinople

C ◆ 1043
survivors attempt to return home overland but are captured or killed at Varna

◆ 922
Arab merchant Ibn Fadlan meets Rus slave traders

◆ 971
Svyatoslav sacks Itil, permanently destroying Khazar power

1041 ◆
Ingvar killed as his expedition ends in disaster somewhere in central Asia

◆ 972
Svyatoslav ambushed and killed by Pechenegs

◆ July 971
Svyatoslav abandons attempt to conquer Bulgaria after defeat by Byzantines

Barda 943 ◆
Rus sack and hold Barda for several months in face of Muslim counter-attacks. They withdraw after an epidemic breaks out

Dvina

Lake Onega

Lake Ladoga

Baltic Sea

Beloozero

Staraja Ladoga

Novgorod

Pskov

Isborsk

Nieman

Polotsk

Vitebsk

Dvina

Smolensk

Dnieper

Loval

Volga

Yaroslavl

Murum

Ryazan

Bulgar

Bulgars

Ural

Volga

Don

Bereste

Turov

Pripet

Chernigov

Kiev

Pereyaslavl

Bug

Donets

Sarkel

Itil

Pechenegs

Khazars

Caspian Sea

Dniester

Tmutorokan

Bulgars

Pereyslavets

Dorostul

Danube

Preslav

Varna

C

A, B

Black Sea

Barda

Philippopolis

Adrianopolis

Constantinople

BYZANTINE EMPIRE

VI: The Transformation of the Vikings

The Vikings made a dramatic impact on Europe, but in the long term the impact of Europe on the Vikings was far greater. Between 1000 and 1200, Scandinavia was integrated into Latin Christendom, but before the Vikings settled down completely, there was one last burst of raiding and conquest.

This final upsurge of Viking activity sprang from two causes. The more important of them was probably the continuing centralization of authority in the Scandinavian kingdoms, a process which was now spreading to the Earldom of Orkney and the Kingdom of Man. Kingship was getting more and more expensive, but royal government was not developed enough to raise regular, reliable income from taxes. Predatory expeditions were therefore needed to raise revenue. The other major cause was the progressive exhaustion after 965 of the silver mines of the Islamic world. This led to the decline and abandonment of the eastern trade routes, and ended the flow of Arabic silver which had been the main fuel of the Scandinavian economy in the 10th century. Renewed raiding in the west was a means to find a new silver supply. The decline of the trade routes and the growing power of Kievan Russia must have made freebooting in the east both less profitable and increasingly difficult, and for the first time, many Swedish Vikings joined the expeditions to the west.

The new wave of attacks concentrated mainly on the British Isles, and were initially old-style small scale pirate raids on vulnerable coastal communities

Below: These 12th-century walrus ivory chesspieces were found on the island of Lewis in the Outer Hebrides. This group—the king and his consort, supported by the church and the warrior aristocracy—is a microcosm of the early medieval Scandinavian state.

Above: The suppression of piracy in the Baltic by the 12th-century Scandinavian kings aided trade and led to the growth of new towns such as Visby on Gotland.

in Ireland, Wales and western England. The main source of these raids was the Norse settlements in the northern and western isles of Scotland, and they would continue into the 12th and 13th centuries, long after the end of Viking raiding elsewhere. This was a region of highly fragmented and competing power structures: in Ireland, the many petty kingdoms and the independent Norse towns; the Welsh principalities; the Kingdom and Man and the Isles and its rival the Earldom of Orkney. It was also an arena for competition between the emerging centralized kingdoms of England, Scotland and Norway, which all had ambitions to extend their authority into the area. In such circumstances Viking freebooters like Svein Asleifarson from Orkney could prosper after they had been suppressed in more settled areas. Apart from occasional royal forays, such as King Magnus Barelegs's expedition in 1098, these raids had no political objectives, and were merely an unpleasant nuisance. Neither in England, Wales nor Ireland did they threaten any permanent Viking conquest: only in Scotland were any territorial gains made.

The same could not be said of the raids on eastern England from Denmark and Norway. These too started out as small-scale pirate raids, but in the 990s they were escalated by Olaf Tryggvason and Svein Forkbeard into methodical plundering and tribute-gathering expeditions by professional armies. Svein was the reigning king of Denmark, Olaf aspired to the kingdom of Norway, but the new style centralized monarchy was expensive to acquire and maintain, and for both men Viking raiding was a means of financing their ambitions. Olaf briefly achieved his ambition before being killed in battle in 1000, but Svein survived to become the most successful Viking leader so far. Though they probably involved rather larger armies than those of the 9th century, these attacks may not have been particularly

Above: *Pagan imagery
survived well into the
Christian era in Scandinavian
art. This 12th-century
tapestry, from Skog church in
Sweden, shows Odin (on the
left), Thor with his hammer
(centre) and the fertility god
Freyr holding an ear of corn
(right).*

Above: *Though actively promoted by kings from around 1000 onward, Scandinavia was not thoroughly Christianized until the 13th century, when this stave church at Kaupang, Sognefjord, Norway, was built. The stave-building method of construction was first used in the late Viking age for domestic buildings as well as churches.*

destructive—once they had demonstrated their superiority over the English defences, the armies were usually content to be bought off by huge Danegelds, rising from 24,000 lbs. of silver in 1002 to 48,000 lbs. in 1012. Lacking a revenue-raising machinery at home, Svein had become a parasite on the English kingdom's efficient administrative system, which raised these sums without apparent difficulty. By 1012, English morale was collapsing, and in a final campaign Svein conquered the country and was accepted as king of England in 1013. He did not live to enjoy his triumph but, after putting down a revival of English resistance, his son Cnut inherited the kingdom in 1016.

The Triumph of Cnut

Cnut's conquest was essentially a political takeover. England saw the introduction of a new ruling class, but there was no widespread Danish settlement as in the 9th century. Even after over 30 years of raiding, England's resources were far greater than those of any Scandinavian kingdom, and though he went on to become King of Denmark and Norway and overlord of Sweden, Cnut's power base was always England. Cnut recognized the institutional superiority of the kingdom he had conquered: he adopted the trappings of Anglo-Saxon Christian kingship and became a generous benefactor of the church in England and Scandinavia. This made Cnut the first Scandinavian king to be accepted as an equal by the other Christian rulers of western Europe—an acceptance powerfully symbolized by Cnut's attendance at the coronation of the Emperor Conrad in Rome in 1027.

Cnut failed to give his empire any institutional coherence; it fell apart after

his death, and in 1042 the native dynasty returned to power in England. However, a claim to rule England was inherited first by the Norwegian King Harald Hardrada and then the Danish Kings Svein Estrithson and Cnut IV. All three intervened unsuccessfully in England in pursuit of their claims: only after the failure of Cnut IV's expedition of 1085 even to set sail, and his subsequent murder, was the Viking age in England truly over.

The Twilight of the Viking Age

In the rest of the British Isles the Viking age faded away more imperceptibly as the Norse settlers gradually assimilated with the native Celts. Piracy and raiding, in ships very little different from those the Vikings used, continued to be a way of life in the isles until the 17th century, but as part of the Gaelic way of life.

After the break-up of Cnut's empire, Sweden recovered full independence, while Denmark passed briefly under Norwegian rule until the accession of Svein Estrithson in 1046. Svein's claim was challenged by the new Norwegian king, Harald Hardrada. Years of destructive and ultimately futile warfare followed, but by 1064 Harald reluctantly accepted Svein as ruler of Denmark. The process of progressive centralization, which had begun before the Viking age, had finally reached a state of balance and would go no further until the Union of Kalmar in 1397. Denmark, Norway and Sweden had become stable territorial kingdoms, each lacking the resources permanently to dominate the others. To varying degrees, all three kingdoms still lacked internal stability. Even Denmark, which had the longest tradition of unity, suffered long civil wars in the 12th century and was even, very briefly, divided into three parts in 1157 after a particularly inconclusive conflict. Norway too was frequently subject to civil wars, but by the mid-13th century it had emerged as the most stable of the Scandinavian monarchies after abandoning the traditional elective principle which so often led to succession disputes. In its place the monarchy had adopted the theocratic principle which also formed the basis of the powerful French and English monarchies, ruling by right of inheritance and divine appointment. Unity came last to Sweden: the Svear and the Götar were not permanently united under one king until the reign of Knut Erikson in 1172.

A crucial factor in the consolidation of all three Scandinavian kingdoms was the adoption of Christianity. Those kings who first created united kingdoms—Harald Bluetooth in Denmark, Olaf Tryggvason and Olaf Haraldsson in Norway and Olof Skötkonung in Sweden—were all remembered as much for their missionary activities as for their other achievements. Christianity had many advantages for a king intent on centralizing authority in his kingdom. Christianity brought a new ideology of divinely ordained kingship which helped to raise the king above his subjects. Conversion also made relations with the Christian kingdoms of western Europe easier. The church brought with it able and literate administrators who could help in the creation of effective royal governments. The foundation of bishoprics helped not only the propagation of the faith, but also created new administrative centres. An efficiently administered kingdom made the raising of revenue from taxes, tolls and fines easier and more reliable, and reduced the king's dependence on more hazardous means of acquiring wealth such as plundering expeditions. The growth of royal government also offered the ambitious a peaceful route to the acquisition of wealth and status through service to the crown: the process of centralization which had originally made Viking raiding so attractive as a means to these ends had by the late

Left: Viking influence persisted in England long after the Vikings had ceased to be a threat. This Norman archway at Kilpeck church, Herefordshire, is extravagantly decorated in the late-Viking Urnes style.

11th century made it unneccessary.

Though the church was jealous of its spiritual authority and could sometimes bring unwelcome interference in internal affairs from the papacy, it was aware that a strong monarchy made its own task of conversion easier, and kings could usually rely on the church to help increase royal authority. The boundaries of bishoprics and archbishoprics helped to define the borders of the Scandinavian kingdoms. For example, the archbishopric of Uppsala founded in 1164 included the bishoprics of both Svealand and Götaland as well as the bishopric of Åbo in Finland, prefiguring by some years the boundaries of the medieval Swedish kingdom. By replacing a diversity of local practices and beliefs with a uniform religion, Christianity could also act as a unifying influence and help create a common identity. However, it would be the late 12th century before the Scandinavian kingdoms were thoroughly Christianized. While those who were anxious for political advancement were quick to follow their kings' examples, paganism lingered among the ordinary people, especially in Sweden where the great cult centre at Uppsala, only 18 miles (30 km) from the royal Christian centre at Sigtuna, was probably still in use as late as 1110.

Below: The death of Olaf Haraldsson at the Battle of Stikelstad in 1030, from a 13th-century Icelandic manuscript. Olaf actively promoted Christianity among his sujbects; the brutality of his methods was no obstacle to his canonization soon after his death.

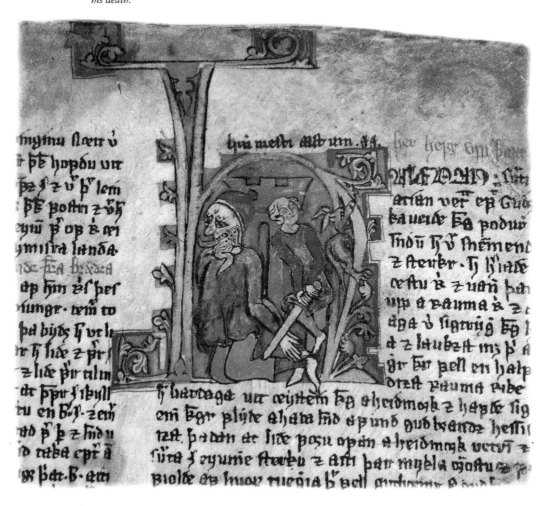

Europe's Last Pagans

Scandinavian expansion, which had come to an end after Cnut's triumph, began again towards the middle of the 12th century. The kingdoms of western Europe were now too strong to challenge, but south and east of the Baltic were the still pagan west Slavs or Wends and the Baltic and Finnic peoples. The Wends were active and skilled pirates, and the Danes in particular had suffered greatly from their Viking-style raids. At least to begin with, it was self-defence as much as religious fervour that led the Danes and the Swedes to become involved in the crusades to conquer and convert Europe's last pagans. The Norwegians too turned their energies to crusading, but were more likely to go to the Holy Land. Although many of the campaigns in the Baltic were indistinguishable from Viking raids in the tactics employed, they were an integral part of the wider European crusading movement and a clear sign of Scandinavia's entry into the mainstream of Europe.

Right: *By the 12th century, Scandinavians like this knight on a gravestone from Vejerslev in Denmark were participating in crusades to the Holy Land - evidence of their entry into the political and cultural mainstream of medieval Europe.*

Raids on Æthelræd's Kingdom

Æthelræd, the insecure Saxon ruler of England, was faced by a series of relentless Viking attacks.

"Then one of the Viking warriors let go a spear from his hands, let it fly from his fist so that it went all too deeply into Æthelræd's noble thane."
Anglo-Saxon poem *The Battle of Maldon*

After the fall of the kingdom of York in 954, England enjoyed 26 years of freedom from Viking attacks. But instability in Scandinavia and an interruption of silver supplies from the Middle East prompted a new spate of raids in the 980s. The raiders were numerous, well organized and—in contrast to the Anglo-Saxons—purposefully led. The mettle of the Anglo-Saxon kings had declined after the death of Edgar in 975. His successor Edward, murdered after an unhappy reign of three years, was replaced by his 12-year-old brother, the unwarlike Æthelræd.

In 991 Olaf Tryggvason, a descendant of Harald Finehair, ravaged Kent and Sussex and defeated the East Anglians under the Ealdorman Byhrtnoth at Maldon, Essex. He was bought off with a massive payment of 22,000 lbs of silver, but two years later was back for more, in alliance with the Danish King Svein Forkbeard. Olaf took his money and reputation to Norway, where he established himself as king. Svein returned to Denmark and spent the next five years trying to sieze Norway from his former ally. Danish raids on England continued unabated, however, and another Danegeld, of 24,000 lbs, was paid in 1002. Later that year Æthelræd, advised of a conspiracy, ordered a massacre of Danes living in England. Svein's sister was said to have been among the victims: true or not, Svein was back campaigning in southwest England in 1003 and in East Anglia in 1004. The following year there was a famine in England; Svein and his army, which had to live off the land, gave the country a brief respite, but he returned again in 1006–7 and was bought off with 36,000 lbs of Danegeld.

Above: a silver penny of Æthelræd, king of England from 978–1016. Æthelræd was certainly unsuited to the role of warrior king, but his nickname "Unræd" does not mean "unready"—his kingdom was wealthy, efficient and had a strong fleet. The Saxon word means "ill-advised"; Æthelræd failed to inspire confidence in his subjects, provoked Danish reprisals by a massacre, and allowed his defences to be undermined by treason.

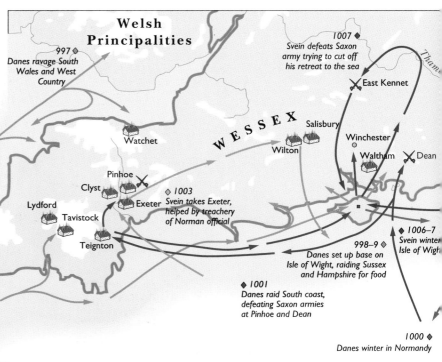

Welsh Principalities

997 ◊
Danes ravage South Wales and West Country

1007 ◊
Svein defeats Saxon army trying to cut off his retreat to the sea

East Kennet

Watchet

WESSEX

Salisbury

Winchester

Wilton

Waltham ✕ Dean

Pinhoe ✕
Clyst

Lydford

Tavistock

Exeter

◊ 1003
Svein takes Exeter, helped by treachery of Norman official

Teignton

1006–7 ◊
Svein winter Isle of Wigh

998–9 ◊
Danes set up base on Isle of Wight, raiding Sussex and Hampshire for food

◆ 1001
Danes raid South coast, defeating Saxon armies at Pinhoe and Dean

1000 ◆
Danes winter in Normandy

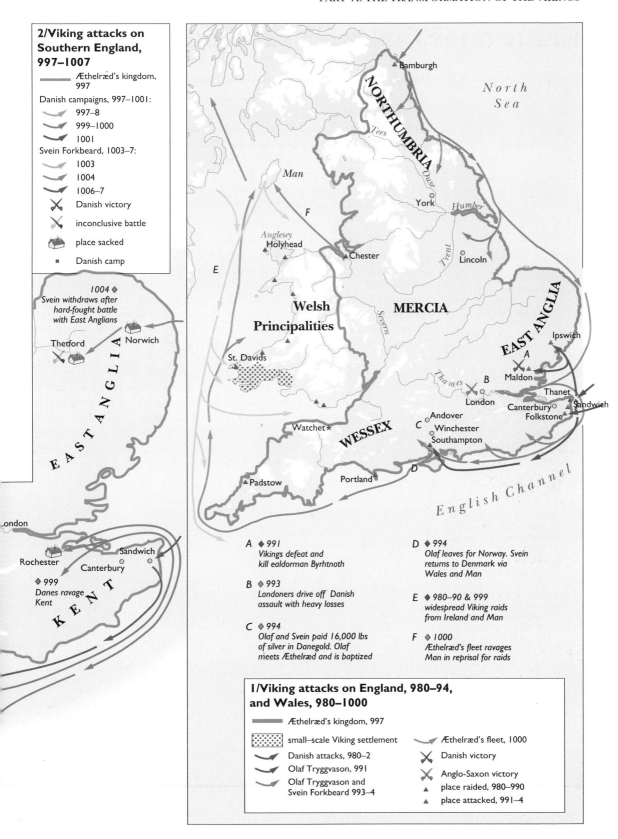

2/Viking attacks on Southern England, 997–1007

- ▬▬ Æthelræd's kingdom, 997
- Danish campaigns, 997–1001:
  - ⟶ 997–8
  - ⟶ 999–1000
  - ⟶ 1001
- Svein Forkbeard, 1003–7:
  - ⟶ 1003
  - ⟶ 1004
  - ⟶ 1006–7
- ✗ Danish victory
- ✗ inconclusive battle
- 🏚 place sacked
- ▪ Danish camp

1004 ◆
Svein withdraws after hard-fought battle with East Anglians

Thetford
Norwich

EAST ANGLIA

London
Rochester
Canterbury
Sandwich

KENT

◆ 999
Danes ravage Kent

NORTHUMBRIA
Bamburgh
North Sea
Tees
Man
York
Humber
Ouse
Anglesey
Holyhead
Chester
Lincoln
Trent
Welsh Principalities
MERCIA
Severn
EAST ANGLIA
Ipswich
St. Davids
Thames
Maldon
London
Thanet
Canterbury
Sandwich
Folkstone
Andover
Winchester
Southampton
Watchet
WESSEX
Padstow
Portland
English Channel

A ◆ 991
Vikings defeat and kill ealdorman Byrhtnoth

B ◆ 993
Londoners drive off Danish assault with heavy losses

C ◆ 994
Olaf and Svein paid 16,000 lbs of silver in Danegold. Olaf meets Æthelræd and is baptized

D ◆ 994
Olaf leaves for Norway. Svein returns to Denmark via Wales and Man

E ◆ 980–90 & 999
widespread Viking raids from Ireland and Man

F ◆ 1000
Æthelræd's fleet ravages Man in reprisal for raids

1/Viking attacks on England, 980–94, and Wales, 980–1000

- ▬▬ Æthelræd's kingdom, 997
- ▨ small–scale Viking settlement
- ⟶ Danish attacks, 980–2
- ⟶ Olaf Tryggvason, 991
- ⟶ Olaf Tryggvason and Svein Forkbeard 993–4
- ⟶ Æthelræd's fleet, 1000
- ✗ Danish victory
- ✗ Anglo-Saxon victory
- ▲ place raided, 980–990
- ▲ place attacked, 991–4

The Danes Conquer England

Above: *Odda's Chapel was part of the Saxon monastery at Deerhurst, Gloucestershire. This was the burial place of St Alphege, a monk martyred by the Danes in 1011. King Edmund, defeated at Ashingdon in 1016, fled to Deerhurst, pursued by Cnut. The two met on nearby Alney Island in the Severn, and agreed to divide the kingdom.*

Sometime between 1007 and 1013, the objective of Svein's campaigns in England changed from extortion of Danegeld to outright conquest.

Unlike the 9th-century Viking invasions, this was a political venture aimed at enlarging royal power and prestige, not an invasion of settlers. The warriors who followed Svein, and after him Cnut, were professional soldiers fighting for a share of the Danegeld. Although many of the leaders and some hand-picked warriors stayed in England after the conquest, most of the Vikings took their earnings and went home to Denmark, Norway and Sweden.

After Svein's departure in 1007, Æthelræd ordered a shipbuilding pro- gramme. Unfortunately his new fleet broke up in chaos in 1009 amid accu- sations of treason, and when an exceptionally large Viking army led by Thorkell the Tall arrived at Sandwich later that year, there was no-one to oppose it. The army spent three profitable years ravaging southeast England, relatively unhindered by a defence that became more and more disorganized. After a Danegeld of 48,000 pounds was paid in 1012, however, Thorkell changed sides and entered Æthelræd's service, for which he was paid a further 21,000 pounds of silver in 1014.

Realizing that English morale was collapsing, Svein returned to England in the spring of 1013. At Gainsborough he was met by representatives of the

A ◆ 1009
English fleet breaks up after quarrels. Danes land unopposed

B ◆ 1009
Thorkell raids Hampshire, Sussex and Berkshire

C ◆ Spring 1010
Thorkell repairs ships before raiding East Anglia and Mercia

D ◆ Spring 1013
Northumbrians and Five Boroughs submit to Svein

E ◆ 1013
Winchester submits to Svein and gives hostages

F ◆ 1013
Londoners repulse Svein's attacks with support of Thorkell, but submit later in the year

G ◆ 1013
West Country submits to Svein

H ◆ Christmas 1013
Æthelræd flees to Normandy

I ◆ Feb 1014
Svein dies

J ◆ Spring 1014
After Svein's death, Æthelræd returns to ravage Lindsey, forcing Vikings to retreat to Denmark

K ◆ 1012–13
base of Thorkell's fleet

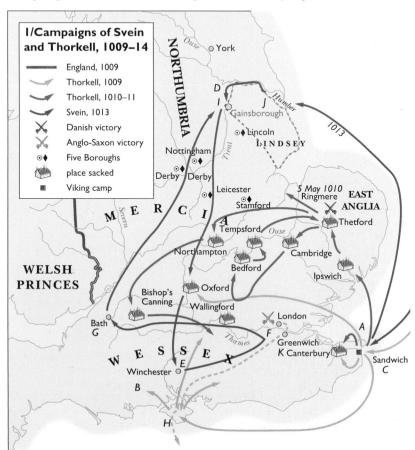

1/Campaigns of Svein and Thorkell, 1009–14

▬▬▬	England, 1009
⟍	Thorkell, 1009
⟍	Thorkell, 1010–11
⟍	Svein, 1013
✕	Danish victory
✕	Anglo-Saxon victory
⊙◆	Five Boroughs
⛫	place sacked
■	Viking camp

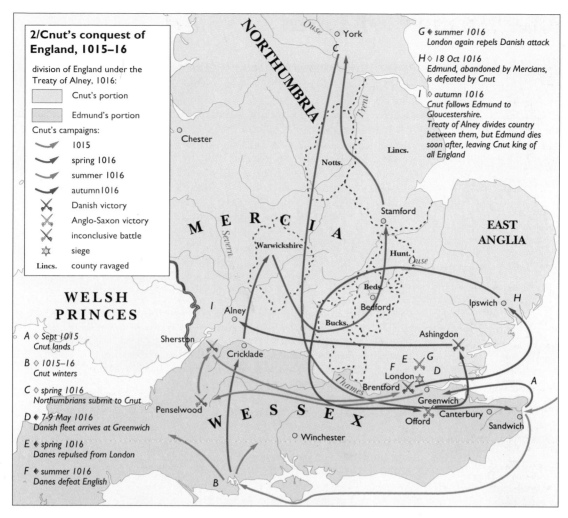

2/Cnut's conquest of England, 1015–16

division of England under the Treaty of Alney, 1016:

Cnut's portion

Edmund's portion

Cnut's campaigns:

➤ 1015

➤ spring 1016

➤ summer 1016

➤ autumn 1016

✗ Danish victory

✗ Anglo-Saxon victory

✗ inconclusive battle

✹ siege

Lincs. county ravaged

WELSH PRINCES

A ◇ *Sept 1015*
Cnut lands

B ◇ *1015–16*
Cnut winters

C ◇ *spring 1016*
Northumbrians submit to Cnut

D ◆ *7–9 May 1016*
Danish fleet arrives at Greenwich

E ◆ *spring 1016*
Danes repulsed from London

F ◆ *summer 1016*
Danes defeat English

G ◆ *summer 1016*
London again repels Danish attack

H ◇ *18 Oct 1016*
Edmund, abandoned by Mercians, is defeated by Cnut

I ◇ *autumn 1016*
Cnut follows Edmund to Gloucestershire. Treaty of Alney divides country between them, but Edmund dies soon after, leaving Cnut king of all England

NORTHUMBRIA

York
Chester
Notts.
Lincs.
Stamford
MERCIA
Warwickshire
Hunt.
EAST ANGLIA
Beds.
Bedford
Ipswich
H
Alney
Bucks.
Ashingdon
Sherston
Cricklade
E G
London D
F
Brentford
A
Penselwood
WESSEX
Greenwich
Offord
Canterbury
Sandwich
Winchester
B

Below: *the end-slab of an early 11th-century Viking tomb, probably of one of Cnut's followers. It is decorated with a "great beast" intertwined with a serpent. Probably made in southern England by a Scandinavian craftsman and found in St Paul's churchyard, London in 1852.*

Northumbrians and the Five Boroughs, who recognized him as king. When he marched south, Oxford, Winchester and Bath submitted. Only London —assisted by Thorkell—held out, but when Æthelræd fled to Normandy after Christmas 1013, it too surrendered.

Five weeks later Svein died. Æthelræd returned to England and the Viking army, now led by Svein's inexperienced son Cnut, withdrew to Denmark. Supported by Thorkell, who had changed sides again, and another great warrior, Erik of Hlaðir, Cnut returned in 1015. He wintered at Poole Harbour, and in spring 1016 marched north to take control of Northumbria. In April King Æthelræd died, and was succeeded by his able son Edmund Ironside, who rallied the English to renewed resistance. Throughout the summer and autumn, he fought Cnut across the breadth of southern England. Finally, at Ashingdon in Essex, Edmund was betrayed on the field of battle by the Ealdorman of the Mercians and crushingly defeated. Cnut pursued Edmund to Gloucestershire, where the two agreed to share the kingdom. When Edmund died a few weeks later, Cnut became master of the whole of England.

The Empire of Cnut

Cnut ruled England firmly and effectively, but found it harder to build a Scandinavian empire.

> *"Cnut was exceptionally tall and strong, and the handsomest of men except for his nose, which was thin, high-set and rather hooked. He had a fair complexion and a fine thick head of hair. His eyes were better than those of other men, being both more handsome and keener-sighted. He was a generous man, a great warrior, valiant, victorious and the happiest of men in style and grandeur."*
>
> Kyntlinga Saga, mid-13th century

If Cnut expected to be accepted as king when he returned to Denmark in 1014 after the death of his father Svein, he was disappointed; the Danes had already chosen his brother Harald. Deprived of a kingdom at home, Cnut returned to England. By the end of 1016, he had conquered the whole country (▶ *page 120–21*). Three years later Harald died, and Cnut went to Denmark to secure his succession. Leaving a regent to rule the country, he returned to England, which he always recognized as his most important possession. He consolidated his hold there by granting lands and titles to his followers, establishing a new Anglo-Danish aristocracy. Otherwise, he ruled in the Anglo-Saxon tradition and made few changes. He taxed the English heavily to support his housecarles (bodyguards) and to fund a standing fleet, but his rule was not unpopular; he was remembered as a strong king who supported the church, legislated wisely and kept the peace.

One of Cnut's chief aides was Erik, earl of Hlaðir, the pro-Danish ruler of the Trondelag. His absence in England gave Olaf Haraldson, a Norwegian of royal blood with a successful Viking career behind him, the chance to defeat the pro-Danish forces in Norway and make himself king in 1016. When Olaf allied with the Swedes and invaded Skåne in 1026, Cnut could no longer ignore him. In 1028 he took a fleet of 50 ships, picked up reinforcements in Denmark, and invaded Norway. Olaf, whose hard-line imposition of Christianity had made him unpopular, fled to Sweden. Two years later he returned, but was defeated and killed by the Norwegians at Stikelstad. Cnut appointed his English concubine Aelfgifu as regent, but she became so unpopular that his grip on Norway began to slip.

Cnut was arguably the greatest of the Viking kings, but his empire fell apart as soon as he died in 1035. His son and chosen heir Harthacnut was accepted as king in Denmark, but the English chose his brother Harald, while the Norwegians crowned Magnus the Good, the son of Cnut's old enemy Olaf. When Harald died in 1039, Harthacnut was finally able to make good his claim to rule England. After his death in 1042, Aethelred's son Edward returned from exile in Normandy, and the line of Wessex was restored.

Earldom of Orkney

Kingdom of Scotland

North

Irish Sea

Kingdom of England

Welsh Principalities

1016 ◆ Cnut defeats Edmund at Ashingdon and takes control of England north of the Thames

London

Thames

Winchester

1026 ◆ Cnut visits Rome to attend coronation of Emperor Conrad II

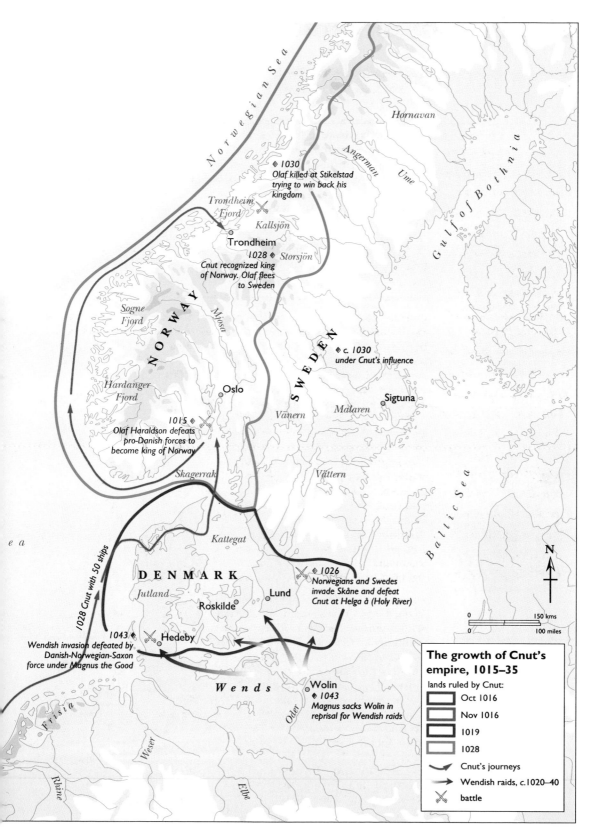

Norwegian Sea

Hornavan

Angerman

Ume

Gulf of Bothnia

◆ *1030*
*Olaf killed at Stikelstad
trying to win back his
kingdom*

*Trondheim
Fjord*

Kallsjön

Trondheim

1028 ◆ *Storsjön*

*Cnut recognized king
of Norway. Olaf flees
to Sweden*

N O R W A Y

*Sogne
Fjord*

Mjøsa

S W E D E N

◆ *c. 1030
under Cnut's influence*

*Hardanger
Fjord*

Oslo

Vänern

Mälaren

Sigtuna

1015 ◆
*Olaf Haraldson defeats
pro-Danish forces to
become king of Norway*

Skagerrak

Vättern

Baltic Sea

Kattegat

N

D E N M A R K

◆ *1026
Norwegians and Swedes
invade Skåne and defeat
Cnut at Helga å (Holy River)*

Jutland

Lund

1028 Cnut with 50 ships

Roskilde

0 _____ 150 kms
0 _____ 100 miles

1043 ◆ ✗ Hedeby

*Wendish invasion defeated by
Danish-Norwegian-Saxon
force under Magnus the Good*

W e n d s

◆ Wolin

◆ *1043
Magnus sacks Wolin in
reprisal for Wendish raids*

Frisia

Oder

Weser

Elbe

Rhine

The growth of Cnut's empire, 1015–35

lands ruled by Cnut:

▭	Oct 1016
▭	Nov 1016
▭	1019
▭	1028

⌒ Cnut's journeys

→ Wendish raids, c.1020–40

✗ battle

The Thunderbolt of the North

Harald Hardrada—the Thunderbolt of the North—journeyed from Norway to Jerusalem before dying in an attempt to seize the throne of England.

Harald's career began at the age of 15, when he fought for his half-brother King Olaf Haraldson at the battle of Stiklestad in 1030. They were defeated, and Harald fled first to Sweden and then to Russia, where he became a mercenary for Prince Jaroslav of Novgorod. Three years later, Harald moved on to Constantinople to join the Byzantine emperor's elite Varangian guard. After nine years' campaigning, Harald had won gold and fame; now he would seek a share of Magnus the Good's Danish and Norwegian kingdom.

In 1044 Harald returned to Sweden. Exploiting his wealth and reputation, he raised an army and invaded Denmark in 1046. Magnus quickly agreed to share his kingdom, and on his death the following year, Harald became sole

Below: *the Varangian guard, the Byzantine emperor's elite corps of Scandinavian mercenaries. This illustration, from a manuscript of the Byzantine historian John Scylitzes, shows them with their Viking axes, three-pointed banners and kite-shaped shields.*

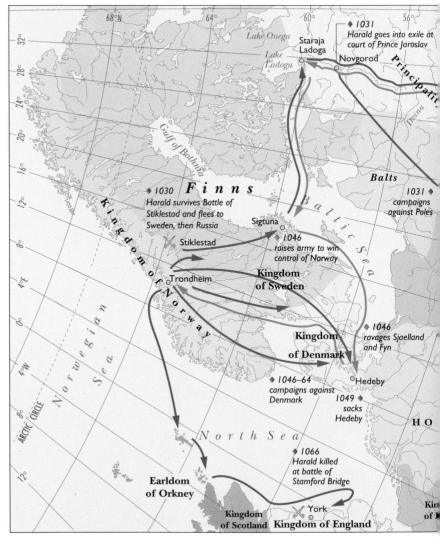

> *"King Harald ... fair-haired, with a fair beard and long moustaches ... He was brutal to his enemies and dealt ruthlessly with any opposition ... but generous to his friends."*
> King Harald's Saga

ruler. But his nephew Svein Estrithson seized Denmark, and years of brutal warfare followed. Harald repeatedly ravaged Denmark, but Svein's dogged resistance finally forced Harald to acknowledge him as king of Denmark in 1064. Harald also faced frequent opposition to his rule in Norway, earning his nickname "Hardrada" (Hard Ruler) by the ruthless means he used to defend his authority.

The death of England's King Edward the Confessor in 1066 led to Harald's last expedition. Edward left three claimants to his throne, Harald Hardrada, William Duke of Normandy and Harold Godwinson the Earl of Wessex. The English chose Harold Godwinson, but both Harald and William laid plans to invade England. Harald moved first. He entered the Humber with 300 ships, crushed the English at Fulford Gate and took York on 20 September. Five days later he and most of his army lay dead on the field of Stamford Bridge: it was said that only 24 ships were needed to take the survivors home. The victor, Harold Godwinson, marched his exhausted army south to his own death at Hastings just 19 days later.

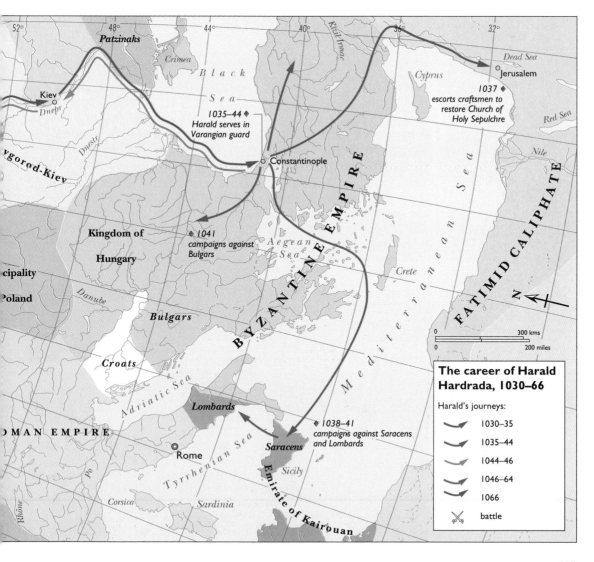

The career of Harald Hardrada, 1030–66

Harald's journeys:
- 1030–35
- 1035–44
- 1044–46
- 1046–64
- 1066
- ✗ battle

1037 ◆ escorts craftsmen to restore Church of Holy Sepulchre

1035–44 ◆ Harald serves in Varangian guard

1041 ◆ campaigns against Bulgars

1038–41 ◆ campaigns against Saracens and Lombards

The Struggle for England

William of Normandy invaded England, but other Norsemen soon arrived from Denmark and Ireland to contest his claim and assist the English rebels.

"As a result of the Normans plundering England... such a great famine prevailed that men... devoured human flesh, horses, dogs and cats... It was horrific to see human corpses rotting in the houses and the streets..."
Simeon of Durham

Following his victory at Hastings, William the Conqueror quickly took control of the southeast, and it appeared as if the English would quietly accept him as their king. Two years later, however, his grip on the country was shaken by a series of rebellions.

After his death, Harald Hardrada's claim to the English throne had passed to the Danish king Svein Estrithson. It was to him that the rebels turned for support, offering to accept him as king. In 1069, Svein sent a fleet of 240 ships to England under his son Cnut and other nobles. The fleet landed at Dover and then sailed north, enjoying little success until it joined the rebels on the Humber. The Anglo-Danish army marched on York and wiped out the Norman garrison. William marched north, but failed to draw the rebels into battle, and headed back to the Midlands to crush a rising. Around Christmas he returned, captured York, and forced the Danes to retreat to the Humber.

William spent the winter in his notorious "Harrying of the North", a brutal campaign of ravaging intended as much to make the area unattractive to the Danes as to punish the rebels. Undeterred, Svein joined his son on the Humber in the spring of 1070. In June, part of the Danish fleet moved south to the Fenlands to join the English rebels under Hereward in sacking Peterborough. But, with English resistance almost at an end, Svein reached an agreement with William and returned home with his plunder.

Five years later, Cnut returned to England with a Danish-Norwegian fleet of 200 ships at the invitation of two rebellious Norman earls. By the time he arrived the rebellion was over, and apart from sacking York he achieved nothing. The last Viking threat to England came in 1085 when Cnut, now king of Denmark, once again planned to invade. By now, though, Norman England had proven its strength and the Danes saw no profit in their king's ambitions. Disputes prevented the fleet from sailing, and in 1086 Cnut was assassinated.

Right: *in this scene from the Bayeux tapestry, William's fleet approaches the English coast. By 1066 the Normans had adopted the French language and culture, but the design of their ships still reflects their Scandinavian heritage.*

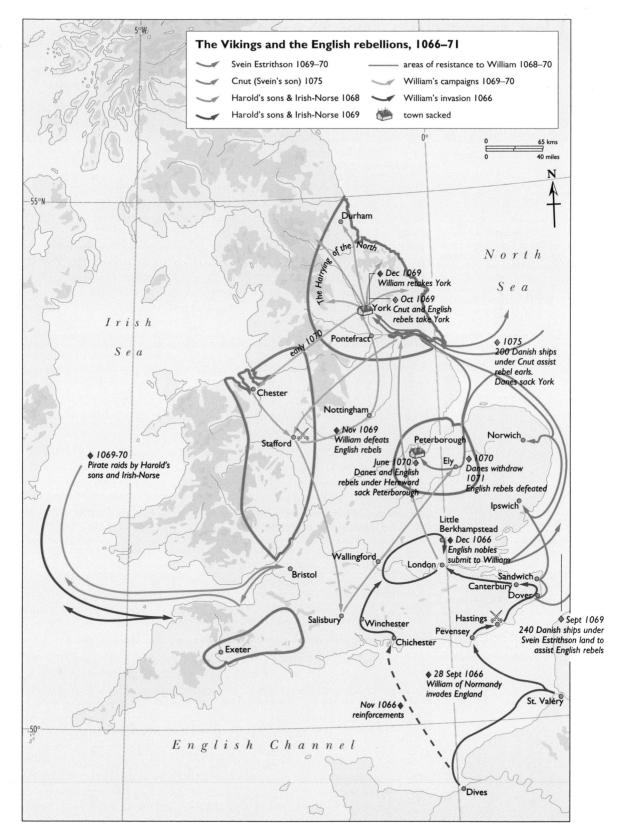

The Vikings and the English rebellions, 1066–71

Svein Estrithson 1069–70

Cnut (Svein's son) 1075

Harold's sons & Irish-Norse 1068

Harold's sons & Irish-Norse 1069

areas of resistance to William 1068–70

William's campaigns 1069–70

William's invasion 1066

town sacked

North Sea

Irish Sea

Durham

The Harrying of the North

◆ Dec 1069
William retakes York

◇ Oct 1069
York Cnut and English
rebels take York

early 1070

Pontefract

◇ 1075
200 Danish ships
under Cnut assist
rebel earls.
Danes sack York

Chester

Nottingham

◆ Nov 1069
William defeats
English rebels

Stafford

Peterborough

Norwich

◆ 1069–70
Pirate raids by Harold's
sons and Irish-Norse

June 1070
Danes and English
rebels under Hereward
sack Peterborough

Ely

◇ 1070
Danes withdraw
1071
English rebels defeated

Ipswich

Little
Berkhampstead

◆ Dec 1066
English nobles
submit to William

Wallingford

London

Bristol

Sandwich

Canterbury

Dover

Salisbury

Winchester

Hastings

Pevensey

◇ Sept 1069
240 Danish ships under
Svein Estrithson land to
assist English rebels

Exeter

Chichester

◆ 28 Sept 1066
William of Normandy
invades England

St. Valéry

Nov 1066 ◆
reinforcements

English Channel

Dives

127

The Kingdom of Man and the Isles

As happened throughout the Viking world in the 11th century, the Scandinavian settlers in Scotland began to develop centralized governments..

Right: St Magnus' church on Egilsay in Orkney is the sole survivor of a number of fine stone churches built by the Norse in the northern isles after their conversion to Christianity. The tower was originally 12–15 ft (4–5m) taller and had a conical roof, giving it the appearance of an Irish monastic round tower.

The process began in the Earldom of Orkney during the reign of Earl Thorfinn the Mighty (1014–64). Thorfinn was an able war leader: he defeated a Scottish attempt to recover Caithness in 1035 and added Ross, Shetland, the Isle of Man and, possibly, lands in Galloway and Ireland to his dominions. Thorfinn's victories brought him enormous prestige and, though he acknowledged the sovereignty of the Norwegian crown, he was a considerable ruler in his own right. Thorfinn was more than just a warrior, however, and in his later years he attempted to give his domains a unifying administrative and ecclesiastical structure. The first Earl of Orkney to be brought up as a Christian, he actively promoted the conversion of the still largely pagan Norse settlers of Orkney, founding a bishopric at his palace at Birsay after visiting Rome in 1048.

After Thorfinn's death the Orkney earldom lost control of the Isles. In 1079 Godred Crovan of Islay succeeded in uniting the Hebrides and the Isle of Man in a kingdom which he ruled until his death in 1095. Godred divided his kingdom up into five regions, which together sent a total of 32 representatives to the annual assembly at Tynwald (from *Thingvöllr*—the meeting-place) in the Isle of Man. The modern Manx parliament is the direct descendant of this Viking assembly.

The independence of the kingdom of the Isles was soon challenged by the Norwegian monarchy. In 1095 King Magnus III "Barelegs" agreed a treaty with Malcolm Canmore, king of Scotland, confirming Norway's ancient claim to the Hebrides and Kintyre. But resistance in the Kingdom of the Isles meant that Magnus had to establish his authority by a brutal ravaging campaign in 1098. In what was to be the last major Viking campaign in the Irish Sea, he went on to capture Dublin and to exact plunder and tribute in Galloway and Anglesey. Magnus's reign brought Norwegian power in the Isles to its peak, but his achievement had only been made possible by his prolonged absence from Norway. After Magnus was killed in Ireland in 1104, Godred's son Olaf revived the kingdom, though he and his successors tactfully recognized Norwegian sovereignty.

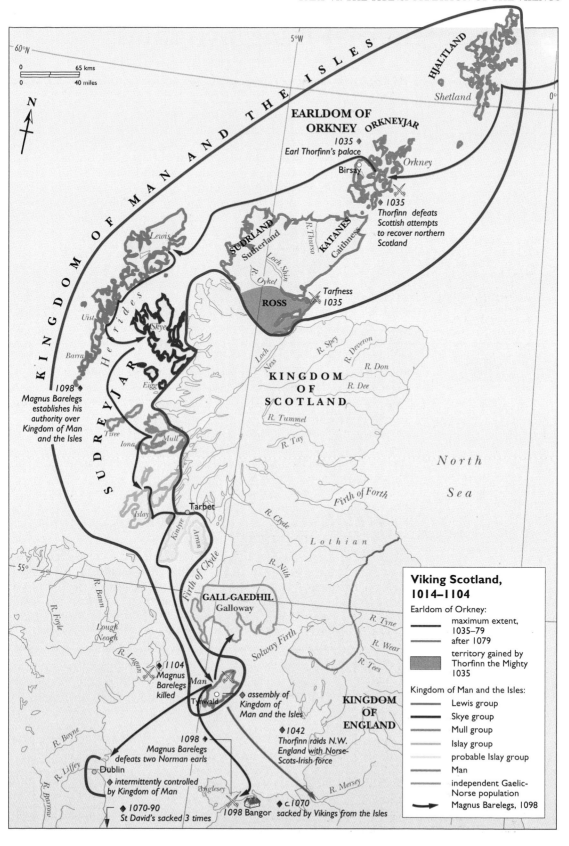

60°N

0   65 kms
0   40 miles

N

K I N G D O M   O F   M A N   A N D   T H E   I S L E S

5°W

0°

HJALTLAND

Shetland

**EARLDOM OF
ORKNEY** ORKNEYJAR

1035 ◆
Earl Thorfinn's palace
○
Birsay

Orkney

◆ 1035
Thorfinn defeats
Scottish attempts
to recover northern
Scotland

Lewis

SUDRLAND
Sutherland

R. Thurso

KATANES
Caithness

Loch Shin

R. Oykel

Tarfness
1035

Uist

Hebrides

Skye

ROSS

Loch Ness

R. Spey

R. Deveron

R. Don

Barra

Eigg

1098 ◆
Magnus
Barelegs
establishes his
authority over
Kingdom of Man
and the Isles

S U D R E Y J A R

R. Dee

**KINGDOM
OF
SCOTLAND**

R. Tummel

Tiree

Iona

Mull

R. Tay

North

Sea

Islay

Tarbet

Kintyre

Arran

R. Clyde

Firth of Forth

55°

R. Bann

R. Foyle

Firth of Clyde

R. Nith

L o t h i a n

**GALL-GAEDHIL
Galloway**

R. Tyne

*Lough
Neagh*

R. Wear

Solway Firth

R. Tees

R. Lagan

◆ 1104
Magnus
Barelegs
killed

Man

Tynwald
○

◆ assembly of
Kingdom of
Man and the Isles

**KINGDOM
OF
ENGLAND**

R. Boyne

1098 ◆
Magnus
Barelegs
defeats two Norman earls

◆ 1042
Thorfinn raids N.W.
England with Norse-
Scots-Irish force

R. Liffey

○ Dublin

◆ intermittently controlled
by Kingdom of Man

Anglesey

R. Mersey

◆ 1070-90
St David's sacked 3 times

1098 Bangor

◆ c.1070
sacked by Vikings from the Isles

R. Barrow

**Viking Scotland,
1014–1104**

Earldom of Orkney:

maximum extent,
1035–79

after 1079

territory gained by
Thorfinn the Mighty
1035

Kingdom of Man and the Isles:

Lewis group

Skye group

Mull group

Islay group

probable Islay group

Man

independent Gaelic-
Norse population

Magnus Barelegs, 1098

The Twilight of Viking Scotland

The Viking age died hard in the Scottish Isles, and raids continued until the late 12th century.

"In 1156 during the night of Epiphany a naval battle was fought between Godred and Somerled, and there was much slaughter on both sides. When daybreak came... they divided the Kingdom of the Isles between them..."

Chronicle of the Kings of Man and the Isles

The slow assimilation of the Norse settlers of the Hebrides into the native Celtic population was nearing completion in the 12th century. A sign of this was the rise of Somerled, a chieftain of Argyll of mixed Scottish and Norse descent. In 1156 Somerled won control of the southern Hebrides after defeating Godred II of Man in a sea battle fought by moonlight on a midwinter's night off Islay. From now on, the strongest influence in the Isles would be Gaelic but, preferring a distant lord to a near one, Somerled and his successors continued to acknowledge the sovereignty of the Norwegian rather than the Scottish kings.

In an area where central authority was weak, there was still room for an old-fashioned Viking freebooter to make a living from piracy. Perhaps the last Viking was an Orkney Islander, Svein Asleifarson, who maintained a band of some 80 followers at his hall on Gairsay. According to the Orkneyinga Saga, Svein raided twice a year. His "spring-trip", as he called it, started after sowing had been completed on his farm and lasted until midsummer. Then, after the harvest was safely gathered in, he set off on his "autumn-trip" which lasted until midwinter. Svein raided the Hebrides, Wales and Ireland, plundered English merchant ships in the Irish Sea and even sacked a monastery in the Scilly Isles. After 30 years of piracy, he was eventually killed on a raid on Dublin in 1171.

By the 13th century, Norse dominion was fading. The Scots had recovered Ross, Caithness and Sutherland by 1202, and harboured ambitions to seize control of Man and the Isles. In 1263 King Håkon IV of Norway led an expedition to strengthen his authority there. His "Great Fleet" quickly overawed the Hebrideans but, after an indecisive skirmish with the Scots at Largs, Håkon withdrew and died soon afterwards in Orkney. His successor Magnus VI, with trouble at home, ceded Man and the Hebrides to Scotland in 1266 in return for 4000 marks and an annuity. Only Orkney and Shetland remained in Norse hands, until they were finally ceded by Denmark in the 15th century.

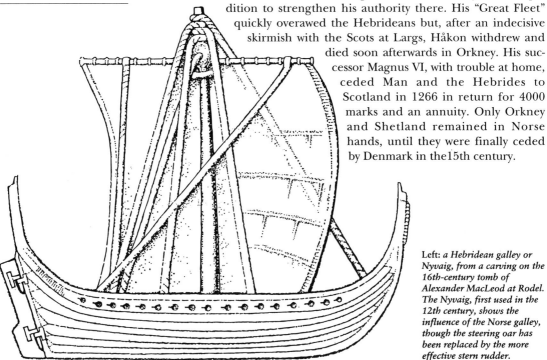

Left: *a Hebridean galley or Nyvaig, from a carving on the 16th-century tomb of Alexander MacLeod at Rodel. The Nyvaig, first used in the 12th century, shows the influence of the Norse galley, though the steering oar has been replaced by the more effective stern rudder.*

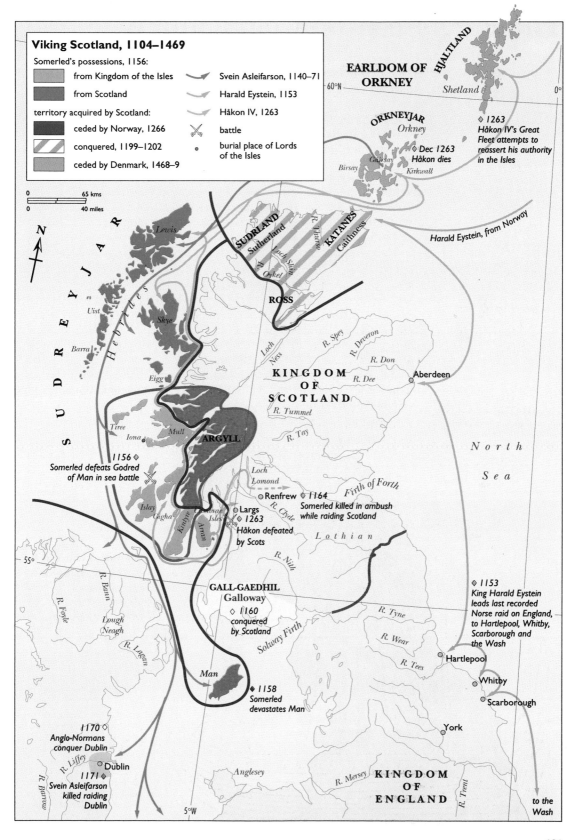

Viking Scotland, 1104–1469

Somerled's possessions, 1156:

- from Kingdom of the Isles
- from Scotland

territory acquired by Scotland:

- ceded by Norway, 1266
- conquered, 1199–1202
- ceded by Denmark, 1468–9

Svein Asleifarson, 1140–71
Harald Eystein, 1153
Håkon IV, 1263
⚔ battle
• burial place of Lords of the Isles

0 — 65 kms
0 — 40 miles

EARLDOM OF ORKNEY

HJALTLAND

Shetland

60°N   0°

ORKNEYJAR
Orkney

◇ 1263
Håkon IV's Great Fleet attempts to reassert his authority in the Isles

◇ Dec 1263
Håkon dies

Gairsay
Birsay   Kirkwall

Harald Eystein, from Norway

Lewis

SUDRLAND
Sutherland

KATANES
Caithness

ROSS

R. Thurso

Loch Shin

Oykel

Uist

Skye

Barra

Hebrides

Eigg

Tiree
Iona
Mull

ARGYLL

1156 ◇
Somerled defeats Godred of Man in sea battle ⚔

Islay
Gigha

Kintyre

Arran

Cumbrae Isles

◇ Largs
1263
Håkon defeated by Scots

S U D R E Y J A R

Loch Ness

R. Spey

R. Deveron

R. Don

R. Dee   Aberdeen

KINGDOM
OF
SCOTLAND

R. Tummel

R. Tay

Loch Lomond

Renfrew ◇ 1164
Somerled killed in ambush while raiding Scotland

R. Clyde

Firth of Forth

Lothian

North
Sea

55°

R. Bann

R. Foyle

Lough
Neagh

R. Lagan

GALL-GAEDHIL
Galloway

◇ 1160
conquered by Scotland

R. Nith

Solway Firth

R. Tyne

R. Wear

R. Tees

◇ 1153
King Harald Eystein leads last recorded Norse raid on England, to Hartlepool, Whitby, Scarborough and the Wash

Hartlepool

Whitby

Scarborough

York

Man

◆ 1158
Somerled devastates Man

1170 ◇
Anglo-Normans conquer Dublin

R. Liffey   Dublin

1171 ◇
Svein Asleifarson killed raiding Dublin

R. Barrow

5°W

Anglesey

R. Mersey

KINGDOM
OF
ENGLAND

R. Trent

to the
Wash

The Early Scandinavian Church

The introduction of Christianity brought new styles of architecture and art to Scandinavia.

The first Scandinavian churches were built by the monarchy and the aristocracy, the same people who in pagan times would have been responsible for ensuring the correct observance of rituals and festivals. The first churches of the 10th and 11th centuries were rectangular structures built of wooden staves. Though simple in plan, these churches could be elaborately decorated as many surviving fragments of carved and painted wood show. The finest example is the spectacularly carved portal of *c.*1070 from Urnes in west Norway. In Denmark and Sweden, wooden churches were replaced with stone from the 11th century onwards, but in Norway the tradition of building in wood survived, and the 12th century saw remarkable developments in the architecture of the stave church. The earliest stave churches were built with their timbers set directly in the earth, and would have rotted away within 25 years or so. However, the later Norwegian stave churches were provided with stone foundations, lifting the church off the ground and protecting it from rot—in several cases up to the present day. Sturdy sill timbers were laid horizontally on top of the foundations into which the vertical staves of the church walls were set.

Below: pagan motifs persisted in the work of many Scandinavian craftsmen who were called on to decorate the new churches. The carvings on this portal of the stave church at Hylestad in Norway illustrate scenes from the Sigurd legend.

The earliest stone churches in Scandinavia were built at Roskilde during Cnut's reign. While native craftsmen could build wooden churches to a high standard, Scandinavia had no tradition of stone architecture or of stone carving (as opposed to incising designs on flat stone surfaces). It was therefore necessary for craftsmen to be brought in from abroad. Stone churches of the 11th and 12th centuries therefore have much to tell us about the ecclesiastical and secular links between Scandinavia and the rest of Europe. Surviving architectural fragments show similarities with eastern

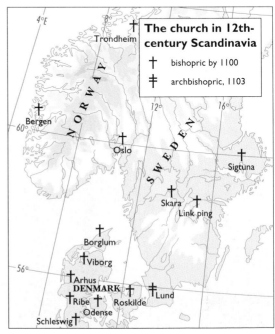

The church in 12th-century Scandinavia

† bishopric by 1100

‡ archbishopric, 1103

Right: stave churches were tall, often elaborately decorated structures with carved portals, verandahs, spires and dragon-headed finials that have an almost oriental look about them; they must rank as the most distinctive monuments of the late Viking age. This one, at Sogne in Norway, was built in the second half of the 12th century

Below: by the 12th century, larger churches in Denmark and Sweden were being built of stone, often by imported masons; Viborg cathedral is constructed in finely cut local granite. Like the cathedrals at Lund and Ribe, it shows a strong influence of the Anglo-Norman and Germanic Romanesque.

English ecclesiastical architecture, evidence both of the origins of the masons and of the English cultural influence Cnut introduced to Denmark. After Cnut's death in 1035, the English connection weakened, and the Danish church came under the sway of Germany. The 12th-century cathedral at Ribe was not only inspired by German Romanesque architecture, it was actually built of stone imported from the Rhineland. Denmark's most magnificent 12th-century cathedral, at Lund (now in Sweden), is an eclectic mixture of German, Anglo-Norman and Italian traditions, showing the increasing openness of Scandinavia to European influences.

Norway's main foreign links in the 12th century continued to be with the British Isles, and the authority of the archbishop of Trondheim extended to the bishoprics of Kirkwall in Orkney and Peel in the Isle of Man. For the 12th-century rebuilding of the cathedral, masons were brought from Lincoln; as a result, the building shows a strong Early English Gothic influence. The style also made its mark on Bergen's 12th-century churches, probably because Norway's first Cistercian abbey at Lyse, south of Bergen, was founded by monks from Fountains Abbey in Yorkshire. Few churches survive from the 11th and 12th centuries in Sweden; those that do show mainly German influences.

Scandinavia After the Vikings

The Scandinavian states became medieval Christian monarchies, and were themselves raided by less settled peoples to the east.

Above: this late 12th-century tapestry from Baldishol church in Norway shows a typical Scandinavian horseman of the time. The period saw the abandonment of traditional Viking-style infantry tactics in favour of mounted knights clad in helmets and chainmail, with short lances and pointed shields.

The death of Harald Hardrada at Stamford Bridge and the dismal failure of the Danish expeditions to post-Conquest England effectively mark the end of the Viking age. Some Viking raiding did continue: the Danish King Harald III (1074–80) tolerated Viking raids in the Baltic in return for a share of the plunder, and the Norwegian King Harald Eystein led a plundering expedition on the English coast as late as 1153. By this time, however, the Scandinavians were more often the victims than the perpetrators of pirate raids. Since the early 11th century, Denmark in particular had been troubled by raids by the Wendish (Slavic) tribes on the southern Baltic coast. These became increasingly serious around 1100, despite reprisal raids the Danes proved no more able to maintain effective defence than the Franks and Anglo-Saxons had to 9th-century Viking raids.

By 1100 Denmark and Norway were largely Christianized, but in Sweden paganism remained strong; a major cult centre continued to flourish at Uppsala, and it would be another century before the country was thoroughly Christian. Denmark was already a united realm by 1000, and by 1100 the strong regionalism which had hindered unification in Norway was declining. In Sweden the Svear and Götar, though usually united under the same king, continued as two separate kingdoms until *c.* 1172. The Scandinavian monarchies remained elective, and succession disputes often led to civil wars in the 12th century.

Despite this internal instability, the Scandinavian kingdoms had greatly expanded by the 13th century. The Danes and Swedes were heavily involved in the crusades against the pagan Wends and Finnic peoples of the south and east coasts of the Baltic. Under Valdemar II (1202–41) the Danes became the dominant power in the Baltic, but soon lost their empire to the Germans. The Swedes began to conquer the Finns in the mid-11th century, and by 1292 had reached the Karelian isthmus, where further eastward expansion was checked by the Principality of Novgorod. Norway lacked the opportunities for expansion at the expense of politically less advanced peoples that the Danes and Swedes enjoyed, but it did extend its control to the Norse settlements of Greenland (1261) and Iceland (1263). Norwegians, like the Danes and Swedes, became involved in the Crusades but their expeditions, such as that of King Sigurd Jorsalafari ("Jerusalem-farer") in 1107, were to the Holy Land and brought no territorial gains.

"Only for their civil wars are the Danes distinguished."
Helmold's *Chronicle*, 12th century

Right: this round church on the Danish island of Bornholm was built in the 12th century, when the Wendish raids were at their peak. Its sturdy, fortified structure meant that it could double as a refuge against attack.

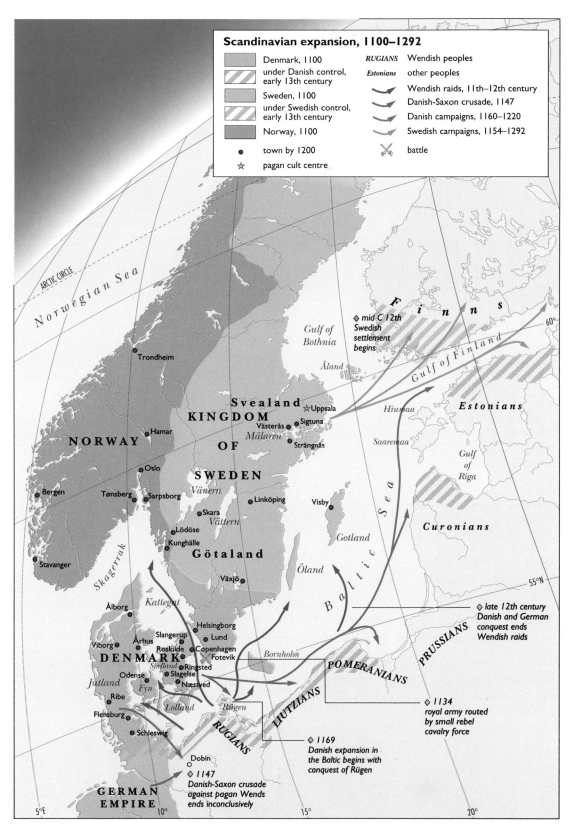

Scandinavian expansion, 1100–1292

- Denmark, 1100
- under Danish control, early 13th century
- Sweden, 1100
- under Swedish control, early 13th century
- Norway, 1100
- town by 1200
- ☆ pagan cult centre

RUGIANS Wendish peoples
Estonians other peoples

- Wendish raids, 11th–12th century
- Danish-Saxon crusade, 1147
- Danish campaigns, 1160–1220
- Swedish campaigns, 1154–1292
- ⚔ battle

Norwegian Sea

ARCTIC CIRCLE

Trondheim

Gulf of Bothnia

Åland

◇ mid C 12th Swedish settlement begins

F i n n s

60°

Gulf of Finland

Svealand
KINGDOM
☆ Uppsala
Västerås ● Sigtuna
Mälaren
● Strängnäs
OF
Hamar
NORWAY
SWEDEN
Oslo
Väner〵
Bergen
Tønsberg ● Sarpsborg
● Linköping
● Visby
Skara
Vättern
Lödöse
Kunghälle
Götaland
Stavanger
Öland
Växjö

Hiumaa
Estonians

Saaremaa

Gulf of Riga

B a l t i c   S e a

C u r o n i a n s

Gotland

55°N

Skagerrak

Kattegat

Ålborg
Helsingborg
Slangerup ● Lund
Viborg ● Århus
Roskilde
Copenhagen
DENMARK
Ringsted
Fotevik
Sjælland
Odense
Slagelse
Jutland
Fyn
Næstved
Ribe
Lolland
Flensburg
Schleswig

Bornholm

late 12th century Danish and German conquest ends Wendish raids

POMERANIANS

PRUSSIANS

◇ 1134 royal army routed by small rebel cavalry force

LIUTZIANS

RUGIANS

Rügen

Dobin
○
◇ 1147
Danish-Saxon crusade against pagan Wends ends inconclusively

◇ 1169
Danish expansion in the Baltic begins with conquest of Rügen

GERMAN
EMPIRE

5°E   10°   15°   20°

Viking Kings and Rulers, 800–1100

KINGS OF DENMARK

Early kings

c. 720	Angantyr
d. 810	Godfred
810–12	Hemming
812–13	Harald Klak (deposed)
	819–27 (deposed)
812–13	Reginfred (deposed)
813–54	Horik
819–27	Harald Klak (deposed)
854–c. 857	Horik II
c. 873	Sigfred
c. 873	Halfdan
d. c. 900	Helgi (possibly legendary)
c. 900–36	Swedish Olaf Dynasty (Olaf, Gnupa, Gurd, Sigtryg)
c. 936–940	Hardegon

The Jelling dynasty

c. 940–58	Gorm the Old
958–87	Harald I Bluetooth
987–1014	Svein Forkbeard
1014–18	Harald II
1019–35	Cnut the Great (King of England 1016)
1035–42	Harthacnut
1042–46	Magnus the Good (King of Norway 1035)

Dynasty of Svein Estrithson

1046–74	Svein Estrithson
1074–80	Harald III
1080–86	Cnut the Holy
1086–95	Olaf Hunger
1095–1103	Erik the Evergood

KINGS OF NORWAY

c. 880–930	Harald Finehair
c. 930–c. 936	Erik Bloodaxe (deposed, King of York 948–54)
c. 936–60	Hakon the Good
c. 960–70	Harald Greycloak
995–1000	Olaf Tryggvason
1015–30	Olaf Haraldson (St Olaf)
1030–35	Svein Alfivason (deposed, son of Cnut the Great ruling under regency)
1035–46	Magnus the Good
1045–66	Harald Hardrada
1066–69	Magnus II
1067–93	Olaf the Peaceful
1093–95	Hakon Magnusson
1095–1103	Magnus III Barelegs

KINGS OF THE SVEAR

c. 829	Bjorn
c. 850	Olaf
980–95	Erik the Victorious
995–1022	Olof Skötkonung
1022–50	Anund Jacob
1050–60	Emund the Old
1060–66	Stenkil Ragnvaldsson
1066–70	Halsten (deposed)
1070–?	Hakon the Red
?–1080	Inge I (deposed)
1080–83	Blot-Sven
1083–1110	Inge I (restored)

KINGS OF DUBLIN

d. 852–6	Ragnall
c. 856–71	Olaf the White
871–73	Ivar
d. 875	Eystein Olafsson
d. 881	Bardr
d. 888	Sigfrid
d. 896	Sigtryg I
c. 902	Hingamund
917–21	Sigtryg II (King of York 921)
921–34	Guthfrith (King of York 927)
934–41	Olaf Guthfrithson (King of York 939)
941–45	Blacaire
945–80	Olaf Cuarán
989–1042	Sigtryg Silkbeard
1036–8, 1046–52	Echmarcach
1052–72	Diarmit
1072–95	Gofraid (expelled)
1095–1114	Muirchertach

KINGS OF YORK

876–77	Halfdan (deposed)
c. 883–95	Guthfrith
c. 900–902	Cnut
c. 919–21	Sigfrid
902	Ethelwald
902–10	Halfdan
902–10	Eowils
902–10	Ivar
919–21	Ragnald
921–27	Sigtryg (King of Dublin 917)
927	Guthfrith (expelled, King of Dublin 921)
927–39	Athelstan (King of Wessex 924)
939–41	Olaf Guthfrithson (King of Dublin 934)
941–43	Olaf Cuarán (expelled, King of Dublin 945)
943–44	Ragnald II (expelled)
944–46	Edmund (King of Wessex 939)
946–48	Eadred (King of Wessex 946–56)
948	Erik Bloodaxe
949–52	Olaf Cuarán (expelled)
952–54	Erik Bloodaxe (expelled, King of Norway c. 930–c. 936)

EARLS OF ORKNEY

c. 870	Rognvald of Møre
d. 892	Sigurd the Mighty
c. 893	Guttorm
c. 894	Halland (abdicated)
c. 895–910	Torf-Einar
d. 954	Arnkel
d. 954	Erlend
d. c. 963	Thorfinn Skull-Splitter
	Havard
	Hlodver
	Liot
	Skuli
c. 985–1014	Sigurd the Stout
1014–18	Sumarlidi
1014–20	Einar
1014–c. 1030	Brusi

c. 1020–65	Thorfinn the Mighty
1037–46	Rognvald (deposed)
1064–93	Paul (deposed)
1064–93	Erlend (deposed)
1093–1103	Sigurd (King of Norway 1103–30)

DUKES OF NORMANDY

911–c. 925	Rollo (Hrolfr)
c. 925–42	William Longsword
942–96	Richard I
996–1026	Richard II
1026–27	Richard III
1027–35	Robert the Magnificent
1035–87	William the Conqueror (King of England 1066)

PRINCES OF KIEVAN RUS

c. 862–79	Rurik (semi-legendary ruler of Novgorod)
c. 879–913	Oleg
913–45	Igor
945–72	Svyatoslav I
972–978/80	Yaropolk I
978/80–1015	Vladimir
1015–54	Yaroslav the Wise

dynasty survives to 1271

Further Reading

MEDIEVAL WRITERS

The Anglo-Saxon Chronicle, tr. Garmonsway, G.N., London 1953

The Annals of St Bertin, tr. Nelson, J.L., Manchester 1991

Egil's Saga, tr. Pálsson, H. and Edwards, P., London 1976

King Harald's Saga, tr. Magnusson, M. and Pálsson, H., London 1966

Njal's Saga, tr. Magnusson, M. and Pálsson, H., London 1960

Orkneyinga Saga, tr. Magnusson, M. and Pálsson, H., London 1978

The Vinland Sagas, tr. Magnusson, M. and Pálsson, H., London 1965

MODERN SOURCES

The following is a selective list, mainly concentrating on recent works which should be readily available to the general reader. Other works and articles can be traced through the bibliographies of these works: Roesdahl & Wilson (1992) and Graham-Campbell (1994) have particularly useful, up-to-date, thematically-organized bibliographies.

Byock, J.L., *Medieval Iceland*, Berkeley and Los Angeles 1988

Bates, D., *Normandy Before 1066*, London 1982

Brisbane, M. (ed.) *The Archaeology of Novgorod, Russia*, Woodbridge 1992

Brønsted, J., *The Vikings*, Harmondsworth 1960

Clarke, H. and Ambrosiani, B., *Towns in the Viking Age*, Leicester 1991

Crawford, B.E., *Scandinavian Scotland*, Leicester 1987

Crumlin-Pederson, O. *From Viking Ships to Hanseatic Cogs*, Greenwich 1983

Crumlin-Pederson, O. *Aspects of Maritime Scandinavia AD 200–1200*, Roskilde 1990

Dahl, S., "The Norse Settlement of the Faeroe Islands" in *Medieval Archaeology XIV*, 1970

Ellis Davidson, H.R., *Gods and Myths of Northern Europe*, London 1964

Ellis Davidson, H.R., *The Viking Road to Byzantium*, London 1976

Farrel, R.T., (ed.) *The Vikings*, London and Chichester 1982

Fell, C.E. (ed.) *The Viking Age in the Isle of Man*, London 1983

Foote, P.G. and Wilson, D.M., *The Viking Achievement*, (rev. ed.) London 1980

Glob, P.V., *The Bog People: Iron Age Man Preserved*, London 1969

Graham-Campbell, J., *The Viking World*, (rev. ed.) London 1989

Graham-Campbell, J. (ed.), *Cultural Atlas of the Viking World*, Amsterdam 1994

Hagen, A., *Norway*, London 1967

Hall, R.A., *The Viking Dig: The Excavations at York*, York 1984

Hall, R.A., *Viking Age Archaeology in Britain and Ireland*, Princes Risborough 1990

Haywood, J., *Dark Age Naval Power*, London 1991

Hedeager, L., *Iron-Age Societies: From Tribe to State in Northern Europe 500 BC–AD 700*, Oxford 1992

Hill, D., *An Atlas of Anglo-Saxon England*, Oxford 1981

Jesch, J., *Women in the Viking Age*, Woodbridge 1991

Jones, G., *A History of the Vikings*, Oxford 1968

Jones, G., *The Norse Atlantic Saga*, (rev. ed.) Oxford 1968

Keynes, S. and Lapidge, M., *Alfred the Great*, Harmondsworth 1983

Logan, F.D., *The Vikings in History*, London 1983

McGrail, S., *Ancient Boats in North-West Europe*, London 1987

O'Corráin, D., *Ireland Before the Normans*, Dublin 1972

Olsen, O. and Crumlin-Pedersen, O., *Five Viking Ships from Roskilde Fjord*, Roskilde 1979

Price, N., *The Vikings in Brittany*, Viking Society for Northern Research, Saga Book XXII, 1986–89, pp.319–440

Richards, J.D., *Viking Age England*, London 1991

Ritchie, A., *Viking Scotland*, London 1993

Roesdahl, E., *Viking Age Denmark*, London 1982

Roesdahl, E., *The Vikings*, London 1991

Roesdahl, E., and Wilson, D.M. (eds.), *From Viking to Crusader: Scandinavia and Europe 800–1200*, Copenhagen 1992

Sawyer, P.H., *The Age of the Vikings*, London 1962

Sawyer, P.H., *Kings and Vikings*, London 1982

Sawyer, B. and Sawyer, P.H., *Medieval Scandinavia*, Minneapolis 1993

Smyth, A.P., *Scandinavian York and Dublin* (2 vols.), Dublin 1975–79

Smyth, A.P., *Warlords and Holy Men: Scotland AD 80–1000*, London 1984

Stenton, F.R. *Anglo-Saxon England*, (rev. ed.) Oxford 1971

Todd, M., *The Early Germans*, Oxford 1992

Wallace-Hadrill, J.M., "The Vikings in Francia" in *Early Medieval History*, Oxford 1975

Whitelock, D., *English Historical Documents c. 500–1042*, Vol. 1 (rev. ed.) London 1971

Wilson, D.M. (ed.), *The Northern World: The History and Heritage of Northern Europe AD 400–1100*, London 1980

Wilson, D.M., *The Vikings and their Origins*, (rev. ed.) London 1980

Index

Reference shown in **bold** are maps or pictures. Quotes are in *italics*.

Acknowledgements

Picture Credits

Arnamagnaean Institute, Copenhagen: 94, 95
Arxiu Mas, Barcelona: 59, 106, 124
Ashmolean Museum, Oxford: 66
Bodleian Library, Oxford: 67 (p. 81 W.1670)
British Museum: 39, 70, 101, 103, 118
Canadian Heritage and Parks, Canada: 98
Codex Photographic Archive, London: 68, 78b, 107, 120, 133b
Corpus Christi College, Cambridge: 49
English Heritage: 54
Historic Monuments and Buildings, N. Ireland: 74bl
Werner Forman Archive: 8, 10 (Statens Historiska Museum, Stockholm), 19 (Silkeborg Museum, Denmark), 21 (Universitetets Oldsaksamling, Oslo), 25 (Statens Historiska Museum, Stockholm), 30 (National Museum, Copenhagen), 33 (Thjodminjasafn, Reykjavik, Icekland), 38 (University Museum of National Antiquities Uppsala, Sweden), 40, 41tr (Viking Ship Museum, Bygdoy), 41cl (Universitetets Oldsaksamling, Oslo), 43 (Statens Historiska Museum, Stockholm), 45tr (National Museum, Copenhagen), 52 (Maritime Museum, Bergen), 72 (Historisk Museum, Bergen University), 84 (Viking Ship Museum, Bygdoy), 85t and 85br (National Museum, Copenhagen), 85c (Statens Historiska Museum, Stockholm), 116 (Stornun Arna Magnussonar a Islandi, Reykjavik, Iceland), 121, 132 (Universitetets Oldsaksamling, Oslo), 133t
Frederiksborgmuseet, Denmark: 46
John Haywood: 16, 18, 20, 22, 27, 50, 76, 78t, 86, 88, 90, 91, 93, 111, 113, 114, 128, 134b
Michael Holford Collection/Musée de Bayeux: 81, 126
Liverpool Museum (Trustees of the National Museums and Galleries of Merseyside): 44, 45br
Museum of Applied Art, Oslo: 134
National Film Board, Norway 102
National Museum, Copenhagen: 34
National Museum of Antiquities of Scotland: 110
National Museum of Ireland: 53, 74b
San Paolo Fuori le Mura, Rome/Instituto Poligrafico e Zecco dello Stato, Rome: 56
St Gall Stiftsbibliothek, Switzerland: 64
Ted Spiegel, South Salem, New York: 105, 109
Viking Ship Museum, Roskilde: 29, 41
York Archaeological Trust Picture Library: 108

Quotations

The author and publishers gratefully acknowledge the following translations from medieval writers used in this atlas:

p.22: *The First Nine Books of the Danish History of Saxo Grammaticus*, tr. O. Elton, London 1894; p.23: *Beowulf*, tr. K. Crossley-Holland, London 1968; p.36: *Othere's Voyage to the White Sea* tr. in *Translations from Old English*, M.C. Seymour, London 1965; p.40: *King Olaf Tryggvason's Saga*, tr. S. Laing, London 1915; p.42: Al-Tartushi, tr. in *The Vikings in History*, F.D. Logan 1983; p.44: *Laxdaela Saga*, tr. M. Magnusson and H. Pálsson, Harmondsworth 1969; p.54: *Alcuin of York*, S. Allott, York 1974; p.56: *The Annals of St Bertin*, tr. J.L. Nelson, Manchester 1991; p.58: *Fragmentary Annals of Ireland*, ed. J. N. Parker, Dublin 1978; p.60: *The Annals of St Bertin*, tr. J. L. Nelson, Manchester 1991; p.62: *The Anglo-Saxon Chronicle*, tr. G.N. Garmonsway, London 1953; p.64: *The Annals of St Vaast*, tr. in F. Donald Lagan, *The Vikings in History*, London 1983; p.66: *The Anglo-Saxon Chronicle*, tr. in *Alfred the Great*, S. Keynes and M. Lapidge, Harmondsworth 1983; p.69: William of Malmesbury, *The Deeds of the Kings of the English*, tr. J.A. Giles, London 1847; p.74: *Njal's Saga*, tr. Magnus Magnusson and H. Pálsson, Harmondsworth 1960; p.76: *The Saga of Grettir the Strong*, tr. G.A. Hight, London 1914; p.92: *Islendingabok*, tr. in *The North Atlantic Saga*, Gwyn Jones, Oxford 1986; p.94: The *Hávamál*, tr. S. A. Magnússon, Reykjavik 1977; p.98: *The Vinland Sagas*, tr. Magnus Magnusson and H. Pálsson, Harmondsworth 1965; 106: *The Russian Primary Chronicle*, tr. in F. Donald Lagan, *The Vikings in History*, London 1983; p.108 tr. in J. Brønsted, *The Vikings*, Harmondsworth 1960; p.118: *The Battle of Maldon*, tr. S.A. J. Bradley, *Anglo-Saxon Poetry*, London 1982; p.122: *Knytlinga Saga*, tr. in E. Roesdahl, *The Vikings*, Harmondsworth 1990; p.125: *King Harald's Saga*, tr. Magnus Magnusson and H. Pálsson, Harmondsworth 1966; p.126: J. Stephenson, *Church Historians of England*, London 1858.

FOR SWANSTON PUBLISHING LIMITED

Concept:
Malcolm Swanston

Editorial:
Chris Schüler

Design and Illustration:
Ralph Orme

Cartography:
Andrea Fairbrass
Peter Gamble
Elizabeth Hudson
David McCutcheon
Kevin Panton
Peter Smith
Malcolm Swanston

Index:
Jean Cox
Barry Haslam

Typesetting:
Jeanne Radford

Picture Research:
Chris Schüler
Charlotte Taylor

Production:
Barry Haslam

Separations:
Quay Graphics,
Nottingham.